Christian Education in the Small Membership Church

Other Books in the Series

Christian Education

in the Small Membership Church

KAREN B. TYE

Abingdon Press
Nashville

CHRISTIAN EDUCATION IN THE SMALL MEMBERSHIP CHURCH

Copyright © 2008 by Abingdon Press

All rights reserved.

This book is printed on acid-free paper.

Library of Congress Cataloging-in-Publication Data

Tye, Karen B.
  Christian education in the small membership church / Karen B. Tye.
    p. cm. — (Ministry in the small membership church)
  Includes bibliographical references and index.
  ISBN 978-0-687-65099-6 (binding: pbk., adhesive perfect : alk. paper)
  1. Christian education. 2. Small churches. I. Title.

BV1471.3.T94 2008
268—dc22

2007044507

09 10 11 12 13 14 15 16 17—10 9 8 7 6 5 4 3 2

MANUFACTURED IN THE UNITED STATES OF AMERICA

Contents

Acknowledgments

Working on this book has deepened my love for and appreciation of the small membership church. But, as those in small churches know, such work is never done outside of the relationships that nurture and support us. As always, I am deeply grateful to my husband, Brent Dodge, who so graciously provided the daily love and support that allowed me the time and space to write. I am also indebted to Eden Seminary, the administration and faculty colleagues there, who invited and encouraged scholarship for the sake of the church and supported the time and space needed for such work.

A big word of thanks is given to my friend and colleague Ann Schroer, who so graciously allowed me to draw on her work with children in the church and shared with me the extensive bibliography on children's literature that she prepared. The results of her work are evident in appendix 5.

I am especially grateful to my students over the years, many of whom have served and are serving small membership churches and have shared their wisdom and insights with me. I offer particular thanks to Angela Boyd, Christine Cunningham, Robyn Miller, and Ed Wilson, who took time from busy student schedules to reflect on their experiences in small membership churches and provide insights into the problems and possibilities regarding Christian education in the small church setting. Their help was invaluable.

Finally, a word of thanks to the small membership churches of which I have been a part over the years. Your commitment to the gospel and your vitality for the life of discipleship continue to inspire and challenge me. Small is indeed beautiful!

Introduction

S uper-size it! This is the mantra of our present culture. We super-size meals, we super-size houses, and we super-size churches. Because of this emphasis on size—the larger, the better, our culture seems to say—those of us who belong to and find pleasure and value in the small membership church often find ourselves on the defensive and even feeling guilty because we aren't larger and striving to super-size.

One of the ways we respond to our culture's emphasis on bigness is to try to be like those larger churches. We seek to duplicate what they do, have the programs they have, and shape our life together as a community of faith like theirs. And we feel we have failed if we can't do this. Nowhere have I seen this attempt to be like the big church manifest itself more than in our work in Christian education in the small membership church. We seek to have a Sunday school like the big church's in the county-seat town a few miles away. We try to have a youth group like the ones in the large suburban congregations surrounding our urban church struggling with shrinking numbers and resources. We attempt to use the curriculum materials and to undertake the programs designed for larger settings and to do it the same way as the big church.

Because of our attempts to be like the "big guys," we often miss the creative possibilities that reside in the small membership church for doing the vital work of education and formation, of equipping the saints for ministry. We miss the fact that *the small membership church is different!* "Small churches are not smaller versions of large churches. They are qualitatively, as well as quantitatively, different."[1]

In the pages that follow, we will briefly explore ways in which the small membership church is different. We will take a quick look at the small church itself and consider some of its identifying qualities. We will think together about the essential qualities and consider the basic aspects of this process we call education, especially as it pertains to the small church setting. We will highlight some of these basics, including whom we educate, where and when we educate, how we educate, and the resources we need. In the final chapter, I will name some important principles that will help guide the work of educational ministry in the small membership church.

This book is designed for those who live and work and serve in the context of a small membership church. Whether you are a pastor, a student in seminary or a lay ministry program, a church school teacher, the chair of a Christian education committee, or one called to some form of leadership in the educational ministry of your church, it is my hope that you will find insight and help in the pages that follow.

Before we begin our journey into the exciting and challenging world of Christian education in the small membership church, a word of caution and of hope and promise needs to be spoken. The caution is that there is no single approach or program that will solve our problems and quickly create a dynamic educational program in our churches. One size does not fit all, even if the size is small! Rather than seeking *the* solution or *the* program, we need to commit ourselves to exploring the particularity of our setting and what that means for the deliberate, intentional, and faithful work of formation in our community of faith. The church of Jesus Christ, no matter what its size, deserves our best efforts. To help us explore our particular context, opportunities for reflection appear at the end of each chapter. It is my hope that we will engage in these reflections along with others in our congregation.

The word of hope and promise is that we do not do this work alone. Jesus promised us that wherever two or three are gathered together, he would be with us (Matt 18:20). We are accompanied on our journey. We can take hope and strength from this promise. Let the journey begin!

The Lay of the Land

My husband and I enjoy traveling. When we arrive in a new location, one of our first activities is to get out our maps and begin to orient ourselves as to where we are. Our goal is to get the lay of the land. That's an old idiom first used in Britain in the 1700s that referred to the shape of the physical landscape. Figuratively, we use it today to talk about the nature, shape, or sense of a place or thing.

As we begin to think about Christian education in the small membership church, it is important to get the lay of the land. To do this we need to look at two things. First, we need to reflect on the nature of the small membership church in general. What are some characteristics of these churches that shape their congregational lives? We also need to do a brief overview of education—what it is, why we do it, and what some of the essential elements of Christian education are, no matter what size the church. Once we have developed this lay of the land, then we will have a good foundation from which to explore the ministry of Christian education in the small membership church in ways that are meaningful and appropriate to these congregations.

The Small Membership Church

"When is a church small or smaller? The most common criterion is that it has less than one hundred attending worship. By this standard, two-thirds of the Protestant churches in the United States are small churches."[1] Most discussions about the characteristics of small membership churches begin with numbers. The first defining quality of these churches, then, is size.

But size is not the only quality that shapes small membership churches. In years past, location was another factor. We used to think of these churches as primarily rural or small town congregations.

Today, however, we find small churches everywhere and can no longer think of them as just a rural phenomenon. I personally belong to a small membership church located in the heart of a large city. Many of our older city churches have become small membership churches and are struggling to maintain buildings designed for a much larger congregation.

So, while being small in number of members and located in just about every kind of setting, what other qualities shape these congregations? Most especially, what are the qualities of a small membership church that are particularly important when we think about the work of educational ministry? Six qualities stand out for me as an educator: (1) there's a strong sense of community, (2) it is like a family, (3) traditions run deep, (4) there's a high percentage of participation, (5) organizational structure is simplified, and (6) worship is the primary activity.

As we look at these qualities, we need to remember that all small membership churches are not exact carbon copies of one another. Each congregation, though small in size, will manifest the qualities and dynamics highlighted below in its own unique and particular way. Nor are the following qualities necessarily absent in larger churches. But they seem to be particularly evident in small membership churches and often play a crucial role in the ministry of Christian education.

There's a strong sense of community

Small membership churches are marked by a strong sense of community. What matters most are the relationships among the people, not the programs being offered. People are at the heart of the small membership church, and knowing and caring for one another is central to its sense of mission. Larger churches must give intentional thought to creating within their midst the smaller groupings where people can be known and called by name, but this comes much more easily and naturally in the small membership church.

We all need a sense of belonging, a place where, as the theme song for the TV show *Cheers* proclaimed, everybody knows our name and is always glad we came.[2] David Ray expresses it well when he says, "There is a crying need for community in a society that has grown too big, too complex, too anonymous, and too disconnected. We as individuals and as the church were created for community."[3] In the small membership church, the opportunity to experience and share in community is one of its strengths.

Educationally, this strength of community, of being small enough that people are noticed and known, means we can focus on people-centered education, not program-centered education. We are able to pay attention to particular needs and interests of the congregational members and give careful thought to how we might address those needs and interests.

To do this, however, we must risk giving up our impulse to do it like the larger church, providing education that looks more like public school education with formal classes and programs. As Ray describes it, "The tragedy for small churches was that when they started trying to teach the faith the way larger schools teach ... they stopped doing what they were the right size to do."[4] Building on a strong sense of community, the small membership church can turn to our ancient Jewish ancestors and the early Christian community for images of what education might look like. In a culture that didn't even have a word for *school*, the ancient Jewish community knew about providing "intimate, contagious settings" where faith is caught as much as taught. We see this described in the book of Deuteronomy. In 6:4-9, Israel is given the heart of her religious teaching, the Great Commandment: "Hear, O Israel: The LORD is our God, the LORD alone. You shall love the LORD your God with all your heart, and with all your soul, and with all your might"

(vv. 4-5). Then Israel is told how to educate: "Keep these words that I am commanding you today in your heart. Recite them to your children and talk about them when you are at home and when you are away, when you lie down and when you rise. Bind them as a sign on your hand, fix them as an emblem on your forehead, and write them on the doorposts of your house and on your gates" (vv. 6-9). In other words, surround the people in the daily, intimate settings of their lives with the teachings of their faith, and they will more than likely "catch a serious case of faithfulness."

The early church knew this wisdom too. We hear a description of their educational ministry in these words from Acts: "They devoted themselves to the apostles' teaching and fellowship, to the breaking of bread and the prayers.... Day by day, as they spent much time together in the temple, they broke bread at home and ate their food with glad and generous hearts, praising God and having the goodwill of all the people. And day by day the Lord added to their number those who were being saved" (2:42, 46-47). In intimate and contagious settings, like around a table in a home, they "caught" the gospel, and God responded to their faithfulness.

A strong sense of community is a vital quality of many small membership churches. It is a strength to be cherished and nurtured. It provides unique opportunity for rich and creative educational endeavors, some of which we will consider in greater detail in later chapters.

It is like a family

The small membership church not only has a strong sense of community but also the shape of that community often resembles a family, an extended kinship system. I am always amazed at the web of family ties that exists in the small membership churches I have known. New members don't so much join the congregation as they are adopted into the family. They are introduced to the family stories, the family rituals, and the family traditions. And the more able they are to take on these stories, rituals, and traditions as their own, the more easily they become a part of the congregation.

There is often a warmth and acceptance of one another in these family-like churches and a willingness to overlook certain foibles and behaviors. After all, they are family. Lest I paint a too-rosy picture of the family-like quality of the small membership church, however, we need to also remember the complexity of any family system. Just as the small membership church often looks and feels like family, it also has all the problems of family life! There are the secrets everyone knows but no one talks about. There are the conflicts, sometimes from the distant past, that prevent Aunt Sally from sitting on the same side of the sanctuary as Cousin John. There are the matriarchs and patriarchs who rule the family and function as gatekeepers for anything that happens in the church.

As you can see, being like a family can be both a blessing and a curse in the small membership church. But there is a particular advantage in this family image that plays an important role in educational ministry. Families are made up of generations. I have among my family pictures a photograph of four generations of my own family. It is something we celebrate. This coming together of the generations is something the small membership church can celebrate and draw upon in the work of education.

"Our world divides by gender, age, size, race, religion, orientation, ability, and interest."[5] It also divides by generation. We put old folks in retirement homes and children and youth in schools, and seldom do the generations meet. The church is the one institution in our culture where multiple generations regularly come together. They worship, fellowship, learn, and grow together under one roof. Functioning like a multigenerational family allows the small membership church to be a place where the old can teach the young and where the young can guide the old. It is a place where the one teenager in the congregation can see herself as a vital and needed part of the family, the church. You don't need a youth group to do this!

Drawing on its intergenerational nature enables the small membership church to integrate all members into the life of the congregation and to see each and every member as vital to the life of the community of faith. We can attend to individual needs and interests. The children of the congregation are understood as our children, and we all have a responsibility to nurture their growth in faith. Being like a family invites us to think about how families grow and learn and to draw on these insights as we fashion Christian disciples.

Traditions run deep

Small membership churches have deep roots. Such churches celebrate and guard their traditions as faithfully as they seek to live the gospel. Homecoming or the annual sausage supper can be as important an event in the life of a small membership church as celebrating Easter. Long after she has left this earth, members will remember where Aunt Phoebe always sat in the sanctuary. Sometimes there is even an almost reverential avoidance of anyone else sitting in "her place" out of an unspoken deference to a sense of her continued presence. It is tradition.

I've heard it said that the walls have memory, and this is a good thing, to be celebrated and cherished. In a previous book,[6] I talk about continuity in the life of the community of faith as being vital and important. Holding on to our traditions helps us know who we are and provides an anchor in a culture that seems to pride itself on living only in and for the moment. My observation is that small membership churches are tough and tenacious. They do not die easily. One of the reasons for this is the traditions that provide strong roots to nurture those who are there.

A key purpose of Christian education is to provide continuity. It is to pass on the traditions and teachings that form the core of our identity and help us know who and whose we are. With its celebration of tradition, the small membership church already provides a foundation for fulfilling this important purpose of our educational work.

But continuity is not the only purpose of Christian education. Holding on too tightly to traditions can damage a church and lead to stagnation, sometimes death. It is too easy for the statement "We've always done it this way" to become the last words of the church. In order to survive and be relevant in new situations, the church also must be able to change, take a different perspective, transform an old way of doing something. Christian education is also about change. As I've often said to my students in seminary, to say I've been educated and I haven't changed is an oxymoron!

Even though traditions run deep and are to be celebrated in the small membership church, we must also embrace change and new life. It doesn't have to be an either-or choice. Jesus modeled this in his own teachings. In the Sermon on the Mount in Matthew 5, Jesus tells those gathered, "Do not think that I have come to abolish the law or the prophets; I have come not to abolish but to fulfill" (v. 17). This is about continuity. However, he goes on in verses 21 and 22 to say, "You have heard that it was said... But I say to you..." Change is also necessary. The small membership church can celebrate its many and rich traditions. It can also risk the change needed to be faithful disciples in the world today.

There's a high percentage of participation

In our culture, the synonyms for *small* are seldom affirming. Small is "little, tiny, undersized, slight; meager, scant, modest, not great; inconsequential, insignificant, trivial, superficial, unimportant, lesser, trifling, of no account; mean, petty, narrow, bigoted, provincial; feeble, weak, fragile, faint."[7] We tend to think of something small as being deficient in some way.

In terms of the number of members who actually participate in church activities, however, research shows that the small membership church has a higher percentage of people who actively participate. Fewer people may be on the rolls, but more of them are active in church. This is not inconsequential, insignificant, or trifling! It is something to celebrate!

It is true that there is a smaller pool from which to draw leaders for the various ministries of the church, including education. And we have to be careful about burnout, especially if we create a church structure demanding lots of people to fill lots of positions. But one of the strengths of the small membership church is the way in which people will pitch in to get things done. Recently, my own small membership church undertook a major remodeling of the sanctuary. When it was all over, we were amazed with how many volunteer hours were given to help do some of the work to keep the cost down.

This higher percentage of participation does not guarantee a Sunday school bursting at the seams. When there are only a half dozen children and youth to begin with, a hundred percent participation still does not create a viable education program if we rely on traditional models of age-segregated classes. However, encouraging ourselves to think of an educational ministry that is woven into the life of the congregation and utilizes already existing gatherings and groupings allows us to take advantage of the higher level of participation and involve all the congregation in the call to Christian formation.

Organizational structure is simplified

"It would be unwise, and often counterproductive, to attempt to force large-church ideas, rules, programs, procedures, and models on these smaller congregations. The small church is different! Recognize and affirm those differences."[8] One of those differences is, of course, fewer people and fewer resources. Many small membership churches quickly discover the need for a simplified organizational structure. There are simply not enough people to populate a large number of church committees. Nor do people want to spend their time in committee meetings.

Even though committees may exist, they often operate in an ad hoc manner and meet irregularly. Decision making occurs informally and is done by consensus. A few folks standing around after church will hear of a problem needing to be addressed. Before they get in their cars to drive away, a plan for addressing it will have been formulated and people enlisted. A few phone calls may need to be made, but generally the plan is in motion, and many in the church already know about it before the day is over (communication is generally faster in the small membership church!).

When it comes to planning, in my experience, small membership churches tend to operate on a shorter time frame, and any planning will occur closer to an event. Again, such planning will occur rather informally and not involve lots of special planning meetings. I've seen vacation Bible schools organized through a series of conversations held after church and over the telephone. Just like a family, the members pitch in to help it happen.

Although I value and appreciate the simple organizational structure and am the last person to want more committee meetings, I also believe being intentional and deliberate is vital to successful educational ministry. Christian education is too important a ministry to let it happen by accident or happenstance. This means, then, that planning is at the heart of this ministry. We need to give thought to what we are doing and not wander from event to event or program to program. Planning does not require a complex organizational structure, but the call to be intentional and deliberate needs to be at the heart of our commitment to Christian education.

Worship is the primary activity

Have you ever asked yourself, why the church? Why does the church exist? As I've thought about my answer to this question, I've come to name three reasons for the church. The first is to worship and praise God. The second is to serve. And the third is to equip the saints for ministry. In my mind, worship is at the heart of the church and one of the most important things the church does. For small membership churches, it is generally the primary activity of the church. Such a church may not have an educational program on Sunday morning, and it may have few gatherings during the week. But it does gather for worship each Lord's Day.

David Ray claims that worship is the most important thing that small churches do. He describes worship in these churches in this way: "Worship in small churches resembles a family reunion.

People of various generations and stations in life behave like an extended family.... They come together to praise and worship the one who gave them life and to celebrate the ties that bind them."[9] He goes on to say that much more happens when a smaller membership church comes to worship than just worship. There is "community-building, care-giving, nurturing, mission, church business, and a whole lot more."[10] I would add, there is education!

It is important to celebrate the centrality of worship in the small membership church and to see it as a strength. Also, we need to see, then, that worship is a central context for education in this setting. We need to realize that everything we do in worship is helping to form the people of God, helping them know what it means to be a disciple of Jesus Christ. Understanding worship as a place of education is vital in the small membership church. Giving thought to how we go about education in worship will be an important discussion in chapter 3 of this book.

This list of qualities of the small membership church—a strong sense of community, being like a family, deep traditions, high percentage of participation, simple organizational structure, and the centrality of worship—is certainly not exhaustive of the qualities and characteristics of such churches. Nor do all of the churches manifest these qualities in the same way. But this discussion does give us the lay of the land and introduces us to some of the issues related to Christian education in this context. Now we need to turn our attention to the topic of education itself and get the lay of the land with regard to essential elements of education that are important as we plan for educational ministry in the small membership church.

Essentials of Christian Education

It is a question I have heard more times than I care to count. A student knocks on my office door, or a pastor calls me on the phone. They are concerned about Christian education in their church. It may take them a while but they finally get around to asking the question: "What do we do?" They want to know how to educate in ways that are relevant, that excite people, that work! And my response is always the same: "It depends."

In a nation and culture built on mass production of the same item, it is easy to think that there is a pat answer to the question. What do we do? How do we educate? Our tendency is to believe that just the perfect program or curriculum or model for Sunday school will set everything right. I can see the slight expression of disappointment cross the student's face or hear it in the pastor's voice when I respond with, "It depends."

But it does depend. It depends on how we understand the basics of Christian education.[11] It depends on *what* our concept of education is, what we think we are doing when we educate. It depends on *why* we are educating, the purpose of it all. It depends on *when* and *where* we educate, the setting in which we work. It depends on *whom* we are educating, the people with whom we work. It depends on *how* we think it ought to be done, the processes and methods we use. Here we have the basics, the essential questions of who, what, when, where, why, and how, and they are as important in education as they are to the journalism student learning to be a reporter.

We will spend time in the following chapters looking more closely at the who, the where and the when, and the how. In the remainder of this chapter, I want to explore more fully the what and the why of education, especially as it pertains to the small membership church. I need to say, however, that the answers to these questions won't look the same for all of us. Remember that each small membership church is unique. To engage in faithful Christian education in your church, your task will be to explore these questions with others who share your commitment to educational ministry, letting my reflections here be a part of the dialogue.

What is Christian education?

When I meet with a Christian education committee in a local church, I often begin with the question: "What is Christian education?" The usual response is silence, as though they have never thought about it before. And it is often true, they haven't thought about it before! They have been doing Christian education, or what they thought was Christian education, for years but never really thought about what it is. In response to my question, they have to struggle to define what it is they are doing.

What is this thing we call education? The word itself comes from the Latin, *educare*. *Educare* means to lead out or lead forth, to bring to actuality that which is potential. This image stands in contrast to a prevalent image of education I've often seen enacted in our culture, including the church. The image is one of education as a banking process, where our goal is to transfer knowledge from one person to another, almost like we are making a deposit in the bank. The teacher is the depositor, the knowledge he or she has is the deposit, and the student is the bank where the deposit is to be made.

It is the passivity of this image that disturbs me most. People are seen as simply receptors of someone else's knowledge, not as authentic makers of their own meaning. Education as "leading out" carries a more active image, a sense of process and movement, of creativity, of bringing to birth. A teacher is more like a midwife than a banker, helping students give birth to their own meanings and voice their own understandings. This is what we saw in Jesus' teaching when he seldom provided answers but instead asked questions and challenged people to come to answers that were authentically theirs.

Drawing on the image of leading out, how would we define Christian education? For me, Christian education is a process that leads to knowing about the Christian faith and knowing how to live as Christian disciples. This process involves helping people pay attention to the activity of God in their lives and developing their capacity to recognize and participate in God's ongoing work of creating, healing, and redeeming in our world.

There are four essential aspects of this process. They are (1) instruction, providing information and experience; (2) socialization, providing opportunity for people to participate in the practices of the community of faith; (3) attention to development, providing nurture that helps people grow and mature across the life span; and (4) transformation, challenging people to change and come to new life, moving toward a vision of God's realm of justice and peace for all creation.

The word *instruct* comes from the Latin and means "to build in." To instruct means to build or furnish within with knowledge. Understanding education as a process of instruction reminds us of the importance of providing information, of being deliberate and intentional about what we need to know in order to be faithful Christian disciples and continue Jesus' ministry of justice, redemption, and reconciliation. In the small membership church, we need to think about the ways we are and can be instructing, providing important and necessary information about being a Christian.

Socialization is the process of fitting one for companionship with others. It is not to be confused with being sociable and friendly, or with being able to socialize easily with others. Socialization is an important process by which we learn by being around others and picking up on the values and patterns of their lives. Much of the work of being a parent is socialization, helping a child discover what it means to be a part of this family and what values and behaviors are important. I learned what it means to be a Tye through regular reminders from my mother that just because others did such and such did not mean we did those things. Instead, we behaved this way.

We also learn what it means to be a Christian by being around other Christians, watching what they do and how they respond in various situations. Children often learn appropriate worship behavior not from formal teaching but from being in worship on a regular basis and watching the people around them. To understand education as a process of socialization is to understand the importance of participation in the life of the small membership church in its daily, ordinary activities and events.

To develop means to bring gradually to a fuller, greater, or better state. Attention to development as a part of the process of education helps us recognize the ongoing nature of our growth as Christians. Becoming a disciple of Jesus Christ is a journey that lasts a lifetime. Our goal is not to arrive at a finished state but to be open to continuing growth and change throughout our lives. There is always more to learn, to know about being a Christian. Educating adults is as vital and important as educating children and youth! Whether we have lots of children or not in our small membership church, we still need to help everyone, from the youngest to the oldest, continue to grow and develop in their faith.

To transform something is to change the nature, function, or condition of it. Seeing transformation as a part of the process of education helps us to understand that education is about change and new life. Conversion, being born again—there are various ways we talk about it in Christian circles, but our theological claim is the declaration found in Revelation: "See, I am making all things new" (21:5). We are called to share the old, old stories, but we are also called to make them new in our time and place. Education at its heart is a process of transformation. In the small membership church steeped in tradition, this aspect of education will challenge us to think about change.

Whether in a small membership church or a megachurch or someplace in between, Christian education is the process of instruction, socialization, nurturing development, and transformation. The ways in which we engage in each of these processes may look different depending on our context, but our need to instruct, socialize, develop, and transform is the same. The challenge to those of us in small membership churches is to discover the ways in which we need to be instructing, socializing, developing, and transforming so that our efforts in education will make a difference in the life of our church.

Why do we do it?

Sometimes I think my young grandson Aidan's favorite word is *why*. Many of our conversations involve a comment by me, followed by his instant "Why?" It certainly keeps my aging brain cells busy trying to come up with answers! But it is an important question, one that helps him grow in his understanding of the world and how it works.

It is an equally important question that we need to ask in the church, especially with regard to Christian education. Why do we educate? What's the purpose of it all? Too often in the church we assume we know why we are doing it but haven't really given it careful thought. A lack of clarity as to why we educate in the community of faith can lead to outcomes we did not intend. It's like taking a trip: if we aren't clear about where we are going, we can end up somewhere else.

This lack of thought as to why we are educating reveals itself in the church in several ways. One of the most obvious is the focus on entertainment for children and youth. We think we need to entertain them in order to keep them happy and to make them want to come to church. Now there is certainly nothing wrong with wanting children and youth to like church and to want to come. But if that is our purpose, then we may avoid wrestling with some of the hard questions of faith with our children and youth and deprive them of some of their important faith development. If pizza parties and game nights are the major events for children and youth, then we are missing the boat as to why we are educating them.

So why is Christian education a vital ministry of the church? Why do we do it? David Ray says it well: "The goal is not to entertain or interest people but to help them become authentic disciples of Jesus Christ."[12] We educate in order that people might become committed disciples of the living Christ, knowing how to live their Christian faith in the midst of their daily lives. We educate, as Paul puts it in the letter to the Ephesians, "to equip the saints for the work of ministry" (Eph 4:12). Our goal is to help people develop their capacity to know God and to participate in God's creative and redemptive work in the world.

When we name and claim the purpose of our efforts in educational ministry, we provide ourselves with a plumb line that helps us decide and choose what we will teach, how we will teach it, and what kinds of experiences we will engage in. It helps us to know what we need to do in order to help our people—children, youth, and adults—bear fruit and make a difference. It helps us to know what is worthy of our time and energy and what is not. It has been said, "Where there is no vision, the people perish" (Prov 29:18 KJV). I believe where there is no clear understanding of the purpose of Christian education, the small membership church risks weak and ineffective ministry. Purpose, knowing why we do it, is an essential aspect of Christian education.

Summary

To get the lay of the land in thinking about Christian education in the small membership church, we've talked about both the unique qualities of these churches and about some of the essential elements of education that are foundational to our understanding of this important work. Small membership churches have a strong sense of community. They are like a family with all of its joys and problems. Deep and valued traditions often shape the life of these congregations. They enjoy a high percentage of membership participation, even though the actual numbers are small. With limited resources, the congregations often have a simplified organizational structure. And worship is at the heart of the community's life, the chief activity that holds it together.

The basics of education in any setting, including the church, require us to think about what education is, why we do it, where and when we do it, who the participants are, and how we go about it. These are the essential elements in any educational endeavor. In our reflection on the lay of the land with regard to Christian education in the small membership church, we focused on concept and purpose, the what and the why of education.

We began with our definition, or concept, of what we think education is. I proposed the following definition: Christian education is a process that leads us to knowing about the Christian faith and knowing how to live as Christian disciples. This process includes instruction, socialization, attention to development, and commitment to transformation and change. This definition is intentionally broad in hopes of helping us see that everything we do in the church is in some way helping shape our identity as Christians.

Our purpose for educating is to form committed disciples of the living Christ, people who know how to live their Christian faith in the midst of their daily lives. We are equipping the saints for ministry, to respond faithfully to their baptismal call to be about Christ's work in the world. Any less a purpose seems unworthy of our efforts.

One final note: I don't think the definition and purpose of Christian education that I've named here are unique to small membership churches. Whatever size the congregation, our educational work involves instruction, socialization, attention to development, and transformation. We are seeking to equip the saints for ministry, or as Ray put it, "to help them become authentic disciples of Jesus Christ."[13] What often differs is the way in which we live out our definition and purpose. Small membership churches are different, and those differences challenge us to think about how we lead people to faithful discipleship in that setting. This takes us to the important questions of who, when and where, and how. It is to these questions that we now turn in the remaining chapters.

Further Reflection

1. List the qualities of a small membership church discussed here: a strong sense of community, being like a family, deep traditions, high percentage of participation, simple organizational structure, and the centrality of worship. Consider the following:

• Rank these qualities one to six in terms of how well they describe your church, beginning with one as the strongest trait of your congregation.

- What other qualities of a small membership church would you identify? Where do these qualities rank on your list?
- In what ways do you think these qualities of a small membership church both help and hinder Christian education in your church?

2. What was your definition of Christian education before reading this chapter? How do you think the people in your congregation would define Christian education? Compare your definition and the congregation's with the one offered in this chapter. How are they alike or different? In what ways has your thinking about Christian education been challenged?

3. Which of the four aspects of education—instruction, socialization, attention to development, transformation—are emphasized most in your church's educational ministry? Which appear to be missing? What might be done to raise awareness in the congregation about the importance of all four?

4. What do you think is the purpose of Christian education? What did you learn in this chapter that helps you think differently about purpose?

2

Who: It's All about People!

"T his is the church. This is the steeple. Open the door and see all the people." I can remember saying this little poem and doing the accompanying hand movements over and over again as a child. I have since taught it to my own children and now to my grandchildren. What captured my attention was the last line, "see all the people." I was learning that people are at the heart of church. It's all about people!

A comment I make frequently to seminary students is, "We teach people, not lessons." It is a reminder to them, and to me, that religious education is all about people too. It doesn't matter where we are or what we are teaching, people are at the heart of the educational endeavor. This is especially obvious in the small membership church. We can't hide behind numbers and assume people will be there to take part in whatever is planned. In the small membership church, we have to think about the people, who they are, what they want and need, and what we can expect of them.

In discussing Christian education, it is vital, therefore, to think about the who, the participants in educational ministry. But what do we need to know? What is helpful knowledge about people as we think about Christian education in the small membership church? First, it is useful to reflect together on our general commonalities as human beings. What do we have in common that impacts the work of education? Second, we need to look at differences. What is different about people in small membership churches that affects Christian education there? Finally, one of the helpful ways in which we group people in order to understand them better is as children, youth, and adults. What are some insights we need to remember about each of these groups when we are educating in the small membership church?

Commonalities: How Are Humans Alike?

It is easy in our increasingly diverse world to think first about the differences between people. And it is certainly important for educators to remember that people come in the particular and not the abstract! Humans are complex and multidimensional, and one size really does not fit all. Yet, even in the midst of our complexity, there are ways in which we are more alike than different. There are things we have in common. Although we may reflect these commonalities in different ways, understanding them is important to the work of education. There are three commonalities I want to highlight here: (1) our biological nature, (2) our developmental nature, and (3) our ability to learn.

People are biological beings

My son is a biology teacher and often tells me, "Mom, it is all about biology." My stepson is a physician who on occasion reminds his father, "Dad, it's in the genes." We are all biological beings. We have a gender, which is determined biologically. We have certain abilities and limitations, many of them biologically based. We have lived a given number of years and are, therefore, at a particular point in our physical growth and development. Certain tasks we can't do until we've reached a particular stage of biological development. Certain tasks some of us can no longer do because of a decline in our physical abilities.

It is important to remember that the people we work with in education in the church are biological beings. This affects the way they interact with the world and the way they learn. An example with young children has to do with the development of fine motor skills. Generally, boys develop these skills more slowly than girls, and this can lead to some frustrating moments when a young boy is being asked to cut and paste a highly detailed figure as part of a Bible lesson. He would be far more comfortable acting out the story, using his whole body in big movements.

We need to pay attention to biology with youth too. Some of the recent research on adolescents suggests that they operate on a different internal time clock than adults, or even children. According to their biological rhythms, many teenagers are just ready for some serious sleep when their parents are waking them up to get ready for the day. The lack of energy that the teenager in your congregation has for getting to church on Sunday morning may have as much to do with biology as it does with interest and motivation. Finding other times to involve him in church may be an important educational move based on biology.

Let's not forget about the biological nature of adults, either. Research and experience indicate that both sight and hearing decline with age. Overlooking this reality can become a barrier to older adults' learning. Making sure they can hear what is being said and can see the worship bulletin or Bible study handout is important. Paying attention to the biological nature of those in our congregation is vital when carrying out educational ministry in the small membership church.

People are on a developmental journey

We all grow and change across our lifetimes. We know that a five-year-old is not the same as a forty-year-old. And we know that a forty-year-old has some differences from an eighty-year-old. As humans, we have in common that we grow and develop even though there are differences depending on where we are on our developmental journeys. Being aware of where a person is in development plays an important role in education.

We've already talked about the biological nature of people and can see that where people are in their physical development affects what they are able and not able to do. This is equally true of cognitive development, how we are able to know and understand. Trying to teach a very young child a Bible story doesn't make a lot of sense in terms of their cognitive development. Sharing simple Bible verses about how God loves and cares for them and showing in our constant interaction with them that we love and care for them too is the important work of education with very young children.

By the time children reach their elementary years, we can begin to help them make some sense and meaning out of the Bible stories. What we need to avoid is complex biblical concepts like salvation or atonement. They simply don't have the cognitive structures to make sense of these. We also need to pick our stories carefully because of the frightening nature of some of them. Hearing Jesus talk about the cost of discipleship and separating sons and daughters from mothers and fathers (see Matt 10:34-39) can be very disturbing to a child. Think carefully about what children will hear and how they are developmentally ready to interpret what they hear when working with the Bible with them.

Sometimes there is an inverse twist to the issue of cognitive development when we deal with adults in the church. I have been a part of Bible studies that seemed to water down the scripture and offered simple, pat answers to complex questions. Developmentally, adults have the cognitive structures to wrestle with the hard issues of the Christian faith and are in need of meat, not pabulum, in their educational diet. Knowing we are all—children, youth, and adults—on a developmental journey is crucial in educational ministry.

People are learners

I have a passion for learning. I also have a passion to know more about how people learn. In my study of this exciting topic, I have discovered that human beings are natural learners. It is a part of our basic biology. Although we may have different learning styles and ways we go about learning, the fact that we all learn is an important commonality. At the heart of this is a vital organ we all have in common: the human brain. To understand some-thing about our ability to learn, we need to understand a few things about the brain.

Let's begin with some brain basics:

- The brain is the "best organized, most functional three pounds of matter in the known universe."[1] It is designed to learn.
- It is 78 percent water.
- It makes up 2 percent of our body weight but uses 20 percent of the body's energy.
- It can't store fat, a source of that energy.
- Eight gallons of blood flow through our brains every hour.
- It has one hundred billion neurons, or nerve cells.

Now, why might these brain basics be important data for edu-cators? What role do they play in a person's ability to learn? Recognizing the complexity of the human brain, the fact that it is so organized, functional, and designed to learn, relieves us of some of the pressure we sometimes feel in Christian education that it is all up to us, that we have to make people learn. No, we don't. People are natural-born learners. Our work in education is to help them learn in ways that are brain-friendly, that work with their brains and utilize all the rich potential in those brain cells.

Knowing how much of the brain is made up of water, that it uses a lot of the body's energy yet can't store any itself, and that a lot of blood moves through it regularly helps us see how impor-tant nourishment is to our students and the ability of their brains to function and to learn. I like to think of the water and the oxy-gen that our circulating blood carries to our brains as important brain foods. We need to drink lots of water to keep our brains hydrated, and we need to exercise regularly to keep the blood with fresh oxygen flowing. Students who have sat for some period of time without a drink of water or physical movement will be less alert and less open to learning. And children, youth, and adults who show up on Sunday morning without the benefit of a good breakfast to provide fuel for their brains will not be as ready to learn as we might like. The brain cannot live off the fat of the land, so to speak, but relies on regular nourishment to keep it supplied with the energy it needs.

Knowing something of the physical needs of our brains helps us work with it for maximum effect. But understanding the work of those one hundred billion neurons is at the heart of our educational efforts. If you think that one hundred billion is a lot, it is! It has been said that there are more neurons in each of our brains than there are trees on our planet. Although I think one hundred billion is a number almost beyond our ability to grasp, it does help us see the richness of our brains' resources for learning.

The neurons are key to learning because they talk to one another. Individual neurons connect with other neurons to form what is called a neuronal network. These networks are the structures for learning. By adulthood, we have literally thousands upon thousands of such networks in our brains. The connections between neurons are almost endless. The phrase "fearfully and wonderfully made" (Ps 139:14) certainly comes to mind here.

Neuronal networks are formed by repeated behaviors and experiences. The first time we hear a Bible story, some connections are made in our brains. Repeated encounters with that story will strengthen the connections, and eventually we can say we've learned the story. Understanding how the brain forms neuronal networks provides support for my argument that spending time with the same story when teaching the Bible to children is important if we want them to remember it. Jumping too quickly from text to text can inhibit learning.

In addition to repetition as an important factor in the process of learning, what else is significant when working with the brain to help it learn? The brain uses two important criteria to determine what it pays attention to and therefore remembers. The first of these is *connections*. An area of the brain called the hippocampus plays a key role here. It works as a kind of file manager. When we encounter new data, the hippocampus sees if we already have a file, a neuronal network associated with this. The brain's first impulse is to connect the new data to already existing information rather than create a new neuronal network. It takes a lot of repetition to create a new network.

This tendency to connect raises two important issues for education and those of us who teach. First, we need to give thought to the connections we are making as we teach. If we spend a lot of time talking with children about the wrath and judgment of God, we risk creating a neuronal network about God that is based on fear rather than love. We have to think about the possible connections a person can make with a text or an idea we are teaching and whether this is really the good news we as Christians want to share.

The second issue we need to consider is what connections are already in place. None of us, whether we are children, youth, or adults, come to education as blank slates. Our brains already have neuronal networks in place. Our hippocampus works to connect the new learning with what is already there. Sometimes this can be a problem.

I had a student once who wanted to teach about idols to junior high students, using the text from Exodus 32. What he did not consider was that these young people already had a neuronal network with regard to idols. Rather than the negative image of idols he sought to portray, these junior high youth connected idol with *American Idol*, the popular TV show where *idol* is an image to which one aspires. If he hoped to teach them effectively, he needed to begin with an understanding of how they would initially hear the story. Then he could think of ways to reflect on the meaning of *idol* and help them reshape their connections. The reality that there are connections already in place in the minds of our students, whatever their ages, reminds us that we need to begin our educating with what our students know and not with what we know. If we begin with their knowledge, then we have a greater likelihood of building helpful connections for them.

The second criterion that the brain uses in deciding what it will attend to is *emotion*. Another part of the brain, called the amygdala, plays a key role here. It scans incoming data for its emotional content. It asks a key question: "Does this matter to me?" If the answer is no, and you as the teacher cannot help the student see why it is important and does matter, the brain will be less attentive to the material.

Key here is that it matter to the student. It may matter a lot to you, but it is the emotional significance it holds for the student that counts. Recall my student and his lesson on idols. He needed to help those junior high youth understand why a negative image of idols should matter to them in the midst of a culture that celebrates being the American Idol, or they will probably tune out.

One additional role that emotion plays in the brain's learning process is related to what I call the challenge/threat line. Our brains need to be challenged. Challenge and stimulation serve as brain nutrients. The brain does not like to be bored and stops paying attention in response to it. In our educational work, we need to provide a variety of creative and interesting experiences and offer new ways of looking at things. These provide the challenge upon which the brain thrives.

But there's a word of caution here. If, in our seeking to challenge people, they end up feeling threatened, we have created a problem. Threat diminishes the brain's capacity to think and learn. When feeling threatened, the brain generally reverts to what has been called the reptilian brain, the brain stem and the cerebellum. This part of the brain is designed to keep us alive. When feeling threatened, we usually choose one of three options: we fight, we flee, or we freeze. Just think of a animal in the forest. When confronted with danger, the animal will either turn and fight, will run away, or will freeze in place, hoping the danger will go away. In important ways, we humans do the same thing. When this happens, we aren't very open to learning until we feel safe again.

Drawing on all of these insights with regard to the brain, I have developed some principles that help guide my work as an educator. There are three basic ones: (1) teach to and for connections, (2) remember the important role of emotion in learning, and (3) teach to challenge, not to threaten. Although these don't guarantee that my efforts at educating will always succeed, they do encourage me to take a brain-friendly approach to my work and take seriously the truth that all people are learners.

When educating in the small membership church, we need to remember that the people with whom we work have some important qualities in common, and these will influence our efforts. People are biological beings, and we need to attend to their physical needs, abilities, and limitations. All people are on a developmental journey and will be at some stage in that process. Even though their locations on the journey may differ, recognizing they are on such a journey plays a role in how we educate. And finally, people are all learners. It is a part of our basic nature as humans to learn, and the brain is central in this. Knowing something about the human brain and how it works is important to our educational endeavors.

Differences: What's Different about People in the Small Membership Church?

Commonalities aren't the only thing we need to consider when thinking about the people we educate. We also need to give thought to differences. It's a paradox we have to embrace. People are the same, and they are different. The people who attend a small membership church are, in many ways, no different from those who attend a larger church. But there are at least two areas in which people in the smaller congregation are different, and these shape our work in education. The two differences have to do with numbers and being like a family.

Numbers

Simply put, a key difference between people in small membership churches and larger ones is that there are fewer of them. Although this may seem so obvious as to elicit a "Duh!" from us when we think about it, it is a crucial difference that impacts how we think about and how we do education in the small membership church context.

One of the most obvious ways to illustrate this is to think about curriculum materials designed to be used in Sunday school. Many years ago, I taught a class of six-, seven-, and eight-year-olds in a small membership church. On a good day, I might have five students, but on many days I only had two or three. Yet the Sunday school materials with which I worked were designed for much larger classes and regularly called for activities that asked the teacher to break the class into small groups. Even the suggested dramatization of a Bible story called for more children than I had. I remember feeling very frustrated with trying to adapt the material to fit my numbers.

What do you do if your only children and youth are a five-year-old, a twelve-year-old, and a fifteen-year-old? What do you do if they are all members of the same family? This is not a unique problem in many small membership churches. The lack of numbers is a hindrance to doing Christian education, at least if we use the larger church setting as our model.

And that is the issue. Small membership churches have to think outside the box in terms of Christian education. The difference in numbers challenges us to be creative. If structured, age-graded classrooms are your only image of Sunday school, it generally won't work in smaller churches. Drawing on images of the one-room school or of homeschooling offers greater potential for our context. We will talk more specifically about these models for education in the next chapter on context, but for now we need to see that a smaller number of people invites us to think in new ways about how to structure Christian education in the small membership church.

It also invites us to think beyond our own church walls and consider ways in which we might work with other churches to meet the educational needs of our people. I know of a small membership urban congregation that has very few youth in attendance. And the three youth who participate with any regularity belong to the same family. Just down the street, another small membership church has only one youth active in the congregation. These congregations have come together to engage in some joint educational ministry, and the one youth joins the other three on Sunday morning for Sunday school and returns to his own church for worship. In addition, the four youth participate with a suburban congregation's youth group in other youth-related activities and have shared in projects and mission trips together. This creative engagement beyond what the individual congregations could provide has enabled these youth to grow and mature in their Christian journey in exciting ways.

Numbers also impact the small membership church when we think in terms of teachers and leaders for educational ministry. There are fewer people to take on the responsibilities of Christian education. It is important, again, to think creatively about this. Perhaps we don't need to burden a single teacher with the one broadly graded, Sunday school class we offer for children. Instead, we can pull together a team of people with a variety of gifts—storytelling, artistic ability, musical talent, a flair for drama—and invite them to work together to engage the children in a variety of learning experiences. Although it is important to have a person who will coordinate this, all of the work does not fall on the shoulders of one person. People also find more joy in their work when they are using the particular gifts and talents they possess.

Don't overlook the youth as leaders too. This can be seen as an educational opportunity for them so that they learn as well as lead. Myrtle Felkner illustrates this with a story she tells about a church where a sixth-grade boy was asked to help teach:

> This boy settled a 2-year old on his lap as he told the Bible story to other preschoolers. Later an adult led the younger ones in songs and role-plays while the sixth grader enjoyed himself devising a game that matched Bible characters and phrases of identification, using an electrical tester. (Most farmers in his community have one!) He took this home so he and his parents could review the Bible story. (Would he have done this without "Sunday school time"? Maybe, maybe not.)[2]

Adults and youth working together in this educational endeavor provide opportunity for both to grow as members of Christ's church. Think creatively about the kinds of teachers and leaders you need and how best to utilize them without burning them out.

Everyone is family

Remember that one of the qualities of a small membership church is that it is like a family. This is another of the differences regarding people in a smaller church. Such a church often resembles an extended family where people all know one another, socialize together, know one another's history and personal quirks, and express deep care and love in a myriad of ways. With smaller numbers, it is easier for multiple generations to interact together on a regular basis. As a student once said to me, small membership churches are "intergenerational by default."

Since family is a quality that marks the small church context, then we need to think about how being a family might shape education. What opportunities and challenges does this image provide us for doing Christian education? A major opportunity that comes to my mind is the same as that offered by fewer numbers. We are invited to think beyond a schooling model of education.

Families don't teach in formal, structured classrooms. They teach in the midst of daily experiences—around the dinner table, doing chores together, taking trips together, riding in the car to soccer games, talking things out at a family meeting. My young grandson Aidan loves to help cook, and slowly he is learning how to make cookies, fix a salad, and scramble eggs. I never say to him, "Now we will have a lesson on cookie making." But he is learning just the same! Family education is more like an apprenticeship, where one learns through doing and from the guidance of one who knows the way.

Such an image holds promise for the small membership church too. Our children and youth are apprentices in the Christian life. We teach them by involving them in the ongoing life of the church. They learn by taking part in worship, by engaging in service and mission projects, by praying with adults, and by studying the Bible with adults during an intergenerational vacation Bible school. Seeing the church as family and allowing ourselves to think about how families educate opens a myriad of possibilities for creative Christian education in the small membership church.

We have to think intergenerationally in the small church. Events that involve all ages, like church picnics, an Advent workshop, a birthday party for the church on Pentecost, or a Seder meal on Maundy Thursday, need to be seen not only as fellowship opportunities but also as rich educational moments where people of all the generations are learning what it means to be a Christian, a part of Christ's family.

It is important to remember, however, that this particular difference, "Everyone is family," is not without its challenges. There is sometimes a privatization with families that inhibits conversation and dialogue. The code of silence, "We don't talk about that," can invade the church too and make it difficult to raise challenging issues and have open and honest conversations about differences of opinion. I've sat in some adult Bible classes in small membership churches where people seemed afraid to open their mouths for fear of appearing different or disagreeable. Fear of being rejected by the family kept them mute.

Just like families, a dominant matriarch or patriarch can control what people are allowed to think and express about something. They can let the pastor or Bible study leader know in no uncertain terms that there is one right interpretation to the scripture, and the pastor or leader needs to follow suit. These problems of fear and dominance are not easily overcome, but admitting they exist is the first step in opening up the family table to richer and more multilayered conversation. It is important to create as welcoming and homelike an environment as possible so people will feel more at ease. And it calls for courage on the part of the teacher or leader to make room for differences of opinion and remind people that there is room for everyone in God's house and at Christ's table.

With regard to people in the small membership church, numbers and being like a family are differences that affect how we educate. My hope is that we can see each of these as an opportunity rather than a problem and celebrate this. God is always affirming "the few, the small, and the insignificant who live by grace, faithfulness, and courage. With few exceptions, biblical faithfulness does not come from or result in large numbers."[3] The intergenerational nature of family-like small churches helps us remember that "no child is so ignorant, no adult so wise that they can't learn together and teach one another."[4] Families are our first places of learning. Being like a family offers opportunities for interaction between generations that can lead us all into deeper insights about what it means to be a Christian and to live a Christian life.

It's All about Children, Youth, and Adults

Certainly, it's all about people when it comes to education. But people do not come in the generic. They come in the particular and unique. Sometimes we group them in ways that help us think about particular needs and interests. One of our basic groupings is that of children, youth, and adults. Using these groupings to think about the people in our small membership churches helps us see some of the things we need to take note of when planning and carrying out educational ministry in this context. What are some helpful details with regard to each of these groups that we need to know?

Children

There are three important details I want to highlight with regard to children. Although certainly not exhaustive of issues related to them, from my perspective, these play a role in our educational work. These details are (1) children are the church of today, (2) children are on a developmental journey, and (3) children are active learners.

1. *Children are the church of today.* We've often heard it said about both children and youth that they are the church of tomorrow. I agree that our young people are tomorrow's church. But they are also today's church. Children aren't simply Christians-

in-training; they are full participants in the Body of Christ now. Jesus had to remind his disciples of this when they sought to exclude children:

> People were bringing even infants to him that he might touch them; and when the disciples saw it, they sternly ordered them not to do it. But Jesus called for them and said, "Let the little children come to me, and do not stop them; for it is to such as these that the kingdom of God belongs. Truly I tell you, whoever does not receive the kingdom of God as a little child will never enter it." (Luke 18:15-17)

We need to hear Jesus' words too. Children, however many there are, are full members of the Body of Christ, and we need to embrace them as such.

The advantage we have in the small membership church is that we don't have the temptation to run a kind of parallel church for children with large Sunday school classes and extensive children's programs. Such programs can inhibit large churches from recognizing that children are a vital part of the church today, keeping them instead on the margins and seldom seen in the rest of church life. In the small membership church, we are easily able to include children in the ongoing daily life of the community of faith at every opportunity. The possibilities are endless if we remember that children are the church of today.

2. *Children are on a developmental journey.* Developmentally, childhood is the time when we are working on some important traits and strengths of personality. Among these are the ability to trust, forming a sense of who we are, the ability to take initiative and do things on our own, and a sense of competence in accomplishing something. The small membership church provides a wonderful laboratory for working on these developmental issues.

Because of its size, the small church is a place where a child is known by just about everyone and is greeted each week by the same familiar faces. It is easier for trust to develop in such a context. It is easier for children to see themselves as part of this family, which contributes to their sense of belonging and identity.

33

The stories they hear and the rituals they share become their stories and rituals and strengthen their sense of self as Christians.

With limited people resources, the small membership church also offers opportunity for children to take on necessary tasks and feel truly needed. When they do these tasks well, they develop a sense of competency that contributes to their overall sense of worth and well-being. Contributing to the developmental journey of children is an important part of the educational ministry of the small membership church.

3. *Children are active learners.* One of my favorite activities as a grandmother is watching my young grandchildren. They go at life with such energy. They are involved with their whole bodies in whatever they do. They are active learners. I think this is true of all children and says a great deal about how we need to educate in the church. We need to involve all of the senses in our educational activities.

With limited resources, small membership churches often think that they don't have what is needed to provide the kind of rich sensory experiences upon which active learners thrive. But it doesn't take lots of money to offer creative options to children. I'm always amazed at how my grandchildren can turn an old refrigerator box into a house, a cave, or even a spaceship in which they travel through time. With a little imagination and creative thinking, educators in small membership churches can create exciting and stimulating multisensory experiences for children.

Youth

What do we need to remember about youth when working with them in the small membership church? I want to highlight three important insights: (1) youth are also the church of today, (2) youth are looking for more than entertainment, and (3) numbers are not important.

1. *Youth are also the church of today.* With regard to its youth, there are times when the church mirrors Jeremiah's perspective regarding his own ability to answer God's call: "I said, 'Ah, Lord

GOD! Truly I do not know how to speak, for I am only a boy'" (Jer 1:6). We say to our youth, "You can't do that; you're just a teenager." We treat them like children, as Christians-in-waiting, the church of tomorrow.

While youth are indeed growing and maturing in their capacity to think and make wise choices, they still have much to offer out of their own perspective and experience. The small membership church provides just the right setting for youth to see themselves as leaders and capable participants in the church today. Because of the limited people resources, there is always the need for folks to serve on committees, provide leadership in worship, participate in mission projects, and contribute to the ongoing life of the church.

In my own small membership church, the youth serve as worship leaders, read scripture, serve Communion, help with the young children, and carry out a myriad of responsibilities. They are clearly seen as active and vital members of the Body of Christ today even as we anticipate the leadership they will offer to the church of tomorrow.

2. *Youth are looking for more than entertainment.* Too often we think that ministry with youth has to entertain them. We plan fun events like pizza parties and ski trips and think that this will keep them involved. The small membership church feels frustrated because it can't entertain like the larger suburban congregation with its own gym, youth minister, and large youth group.

I submit that entertainment isn't what youth need from the church. Teenagers are at the stage in life where they are searching, testing, and looking for something of lasting value and importance. They are open to risking and thinking new ideas and thoughts, trying out new beliefs, but they need guidance. They need adults in their lives who will listen and care. I think David Ray says it well: "With all that our culture offers to tantalize young people, they're in need of a place and people who take them seriously and help them establish lasting values and commitments. Small churches are the right size to take youth very seriously and to give them that place where they belong and can make a difference."[5] Small churches are indeed the right size to offer youth a place to know and be known, to find mentors and guides who walk with them and work alongside them and give them opportunities to lead. Small churches are able to remind their youth: "Do not say, 'I am only a boy.'... [Instead] go to all to whom I send you, and ...'speak whatever I command you" (Jer 1:7). Small churches are the right size to engage their youth in the ongoing journey of discipleship toward a deeper relationship with God.

3. *Numbers are not important.* We've already talked about numbers as a key difference in the small membership church. One of the biggest barriers to creative Christian education with youth in this context is our culture's bias about numbers. With the emphasis on super-sizing it, we see the number of youth in our small churches and think that we can't do it. We simply don't have enough youth to offer any ministry with them. I submit that any church with at least one young person has a youth ministry already, whether it knows it or not.

Youth learn a great deal by observing the adults around them, so we are already teaching our young people through our behaviors and interactions. Being intentional about the mentoring opportunities we offer our young people strengthens this teaching. Inviting a young person to participate in various leadership roles, like the roles in worship mentioned above, provides possibilities for learning and growth in discipleship that do not need a youth group to happen. Be creative, and you will see the multitude of ways even a single youth can learn and grow in the small membership church.

Even if there are no youth in the church, there are still ways to engage in youth ministry. There are teenagers in our world who need our advocacy and care. Being intentional about raising awareness with regard to the teenagers in the local schools and community is important educational work in the small membership church. Opportunities for ministry with, to, and for youth abound, no matter the numbers.

Adults

Our final primary people grouping is adults. There is much we could talk about with regard to adults and education in the church. We've already touched on their physical issues and needs and the role these play in educating them. We know that adults want to study that which has some immediate effect on or connection with their lives. We have to pay attention to what interests them, and we have to ask the important brain question: why does this matter to them? Adults want to know what difference this information will make.

Whereas these details about adults are important, there is a primary one I want to highlight here, a detail often overlooked because of a myth we have about Christian education. The detail is—*it's all about adults!* The myth is that education is for children and youth.

Just ask people what they think of when they hear the term *Christian education*. They generally say, "Sunday school" and "children and youth." We seem to have some difficulty in the church associating education with adults. We will even hold Sunday school at the same time as worship, as though adults don't need to be educated and children don't need to worship!

The small membership church has a unique opportunity here. In many of our small congregations, the membership is skewed toward older adults. A large percentage of those in the pews are senior citizens. We can dispel the myth that Christian education is only for children and youth by creating vital and dynamic educational opportunities for our adults. This emphasis is important for our children and youth too. As Ray says, "The most important prerequisite for a church to be alive and vital and for its children and youth to be growing in faithfulness is for its adults to continue maturing in their faithfulness."[6] For too long we have "assumed that by concentrating on educating children, Christian adults will result. Someone said that Jesus played with children and taught adults, while churches try to teach children and play with adults."[7] In educating its adults, the small membership church can bear witness to this vision of Jesus' teaching ministry.

Summary

It is indeed all about people in the educational ministry of the small membership church. It is about our commonalities and our differences. It is about being children, youth, and adults who are all learning what it means to be a disciple of Jesus Christ. It is about celebrating our biological nature, the richness of our developmental journey, and the joy of learning. It is about recognizing that numbers do make a difference and that the difference holds as much promise as problems. It is about celebrating our family-like nature and using this to provide rich and fruitful intergenerational opportunities.

Finally, it is about children, youth, and adults and the awareness that together we are the church of today. We don't need to be entertained. We don't need large numbers. We do need to be led forth in the ongoing journey of discipleship, learning to respond to the call of God in our lives and to live toward God's vision of peace and justice for all.

Further Reflection

1. Think about the ways people are alike: we are biological beings, we develop—change and grow—across a lifetime, and we are all created to learn. Consider the following:

- Which of these three qualities, if any, were new to you? What did the discussion of all three add to your understanding about people?
- What do these three qualities help you notice now about the people in your congregation that is useful as you think about planning Christian education?

2. In what ways has your church dealt with the issue of numbers when planning for Christian education?

3. How does the image of family influence what you do educationally in your congregation?

- Make a list of the ways in which this image could be helpful as you plan for Christian education.

4. In addition to numbers and being family-like, what other differences do you note about people in the small membership church?

- Make a list of these differences.
- Where do you see these differences present in your congregation, and how do they affect Christian education in your setting?

5. What do you think is important to know about the children, youth, and adults in your church?

- Plan one-on-one conversations with your children and youth. What do you discover that you didn't know? What difference can this knowledge make in your educational ministry?
- What is your church doing to educate adults? What more could be done?

3

Where and When: Sunday School and Beyond

I t happens almost every time. I ask people what is the first thing that pops into their heads when they hear the term *Christian education*. Overwhelmingly, the response is "Sunday school." When we think about where and when we educate in the church, our default mode seems to be the hour on Sunday morning that we have labeled "Sunday school." Certainly, Sunday school is an important context for Christian education, but it is a myth that they are automatically the same thing. Assuming that Sunday school is the primary educational context prevents us from seeing other possibilities for the where and when of education in the church.

This myth can be a particular problem in small membership churches. Myrtle Felkner describes it well:

> "We don't have Sunday school," said my new friend. "We just have two or three children." "What about youth?" I asked cautiously. "There are a couple of youth, but they go to another church where there's a youth group." She anticipated my next question. "We just have a class of older ladies. It's not a Sunday school, really."[1]

"Real" Sunday school has lots of children and youth. A few women meeting for Bible study don't qualify. Attitudes like this lead the small membership church to feel frustrated and discouraged. We overlook the possibilities for vital Christian education throughout the life of the congregation. We forget that "Christian education happens whenever and wherever the church meets, eats, worships, works, learns, plays, cares, and serves."[2] It is the whole life of the congregation that educates!

The small membership church that takes seriously its call to educate and nurture disciples of Jesus Christ will pay attention to the various times and places where education is happening. There are at least three such contexts that I want to highlight here that are vital and hold much promise in the small church. These are Sunday school, worship, and events in the life of the church and community.

Sunday School

Although the church certainly found ways to educate without Sunday school for the first eighteen hundred years of its existence, I don't think we should cast it aside too quickly, even in the small membership church where lack of numbers and lack of space can be a problem. Our problem really isn't lack of numbers or space but our limited image of what Sunday school should look like. If we think a Sunday school requires lots of children divided into different age groupings meeting in formal, structured classrooms, then we do have a problem. But if we are able to imagine school in different ways, the possibilities emerge. Two helpful images for the small membership church are the one-room school and homeschooling.

One-room school

One-room schools used to dominate the rural and small town landscape of this country. All ages of children, from kindergarten through eighth grade, met in the same room. As I've heard older adults tell of their childhood experiences in such schools, I'm struck by some of the benefits of this experience. Older children learn by helping the younger ones. The younger children learn by observing the older ones. Each child has an opportunity to learn at his or her own pace. The likelihood of personal attention increases as the teacher has more time to move among the students and interact with children who need it. All of these benefits are possible in the one-room Sunday school too.

What is needed for a one-room Sunday school? Let's begin with *space*. We don't need a lot of space for a one-room Sunday school. But we do need space that has some openness and flexibility to it. Such space needs to have room for: (1) gathering everyone for a group activity like hearing a Bible story or participating in a worship moment together, (2) learning centers where the children can work at their own pace and level of ability, and (3) movement that is important for games, drama, and role plays.

Giving attention to the quality of the space is important too. Remembering that multisensory experiences are beneficial in helping our brains learn, it is important to make the space colorful and visually interesting. Putting pictures on the wall at the children's eye level, using colorful carpet squares to create a reading corner, and, if possible, painting murals on the walls are all ways to enhance the space.

Certainly we need *teachers* in our one-room Sunday school. But it is helpful to think about a teaching team rather than a single adult responsible for everything. We can invite adult members of the congregation, as well as the older children and youth, to take turns on a Sunday morning to read the Bible lesson for the day and talk about what it means to them. We can ask adults with particular gifts and talents, like in music or art, to provide guidance at a learning center. We can pair an older child with a younger child as a kind of faith buddy and encourage them to work together on assignments and class projects.

The important thing to remember is that a good church school teacher is not the one who knows it all. A good teacher is one who loves Christ and is faithful and committed in his or her own Christian walk. A good teacher is one who loves children and understands that it takes a whole church to raise a child. A good teacher is one who loves to learn and encourages that same love in others. There are many good teachers, even in a small membership church. The task of those responsible for educational ministry in this setting is to call forth these teachers and invite them to say yes to the challenge. The future of the church depends on this!

Finally, we need *resources.* Too often small membership churches claim they can't do certain things because they don't have the resources and equipment. I would remind us that Jesus had few resources for his teaching ministry yet managed to be one of the most effective teachers ever. He used what was at hand, like a mustard seed, a lily in the field, or a candle on a stand.

Small membership churches have resources at hand if they but look for them. The most important resource is people themselves. Our people resources are our greatest treasure. In any given community of faith, no matter its size, there is a wealth of gifts and talents waiting to be tapped. There are storytellers, artists, musicians, good cooks, carpenters, jacks- and jills-of-all-trades—all needing to hear the call to use these gifts and talents for God. Once we stop thinking about what we don't have and begin to see what we do have, we will find the resources we need!

Homeschool

Homeschooling is a growing phenomenon in public education. Whereas there are a multitude of reasons that parents choose homeschooling for their children today, as a model of education it is certainly not a new option. In fact, the Deuteronomy passage quoted in chapter 1 describes homeschooling: "Keep these words that I am commanding you today in your heart. Recite them to your children and talk about them when you are at home" (6:6-7).

Using the image of homeschooling as a way to envision Christian education in the small membership church invites us to think outside the box of Sunday school in a couple of important ways. First, it reminds us that parents are the primary religious educators of their children and that we need to help them with this privilege and responsibility. With the emphasis on the home as the context, we can prepare take-home packets for parents and grandparents to use with their children and grandchildren to talk about faith in the home. A good resource for materials for these packets can be existing curriculum materials that can be adapted for home use. Such materials often have Bible stories and hands-on exercises and experiences that can be easily duplicated at home. Holding a parent meeting to help parents think about how to use these packets is important too.

The second thing that the image of homeschool provides is a reminder that children learn, and always have learned, outside formal school settings. I think of my own children and how much science they learned through our visits to national parks. We were a camping family and loved to attend the parks' naturalist talks in the evening and take part in naturalist-led hikes during the day. The outdoor world became a wonderful classroom.

And so it is in the small membership church when we utilize the concept of homeschooling. Homeschooled children spend time in museums, libraries, parks, science centers, historical sites, and so on. These become places of learning. A church can use a local park as the location to talk about the earth and being good stewards of God's creation. Nursing homes, food pantries, and other local social service agencies provide settings where mission and service are encountered firsthand. Such a setting provides increased opportunity for meaningful connections to a text like Matthew 25:31-46.

The image of homeschooling reminds us to think outside the box of the classroom. It invites us to think outside the time restrictions of Sunday morning. It reminds us that learning takes place after school, on Saturdays, and in any place where we can be intentional about living the Christian life and acting in the ways Jesus would have us act. Homeschooling affords rich opportunities to learn by doing, the way Jesus taught his disciples!

Sunday school is certainly one of the places where education in the church occurs. Expanding our image of the setting to include the one-room school and homeschooling provides opportunity for small membership churches to move beyond the limits that numbers and space often place on us and to think creatively about other options. But moving beyond the schooling model to look at other places where education happens in the church expands our thinking even further.

Worship

Too often in the church we think of worship and education as two totally separate functions. We've even modeled this in our physical plants, where we have the sanctuary for worship and an educational wing for education. And sometimes we behave as though never the twain shall meet. We forget that it is everything we do as a congregation that teaches what it means to be a disciple of Jesus Christ.

In the small membership church, it is especially important to remember that worship and education are interconnected and that worship is a primary educational context. The worship service is one of the key places where we learn about what it means to be a Christian. Because worship is sometimes the only time a small membership church gathers, being aware of the educational opportunities in worship and how to make the best use of them is critical.

One of these important opportunities is the very space in which we worship. Context teaches. In the ancient church, before people learned to read, architecture and symbols were understood to be teaching tools that helped people learn something about God and about themselves as Christians. Architecture and symbols are still teaching today. The images in the stained-glass windows, the pictures and banners hung on the walls, the symbols on the altar, the cleanliness and condition of the room and furniture—all of these say something about who we are and what being a Christian means to us.

One of the most meaningful chapel services at Eden Seminary, the seminary where I've taught, is a yearly service when the church history professor talks about the chapel windows. The stained-glass windows on the sidewalls contain images of key figures, both those from the Bible and those from church history, including the denomination's particular history. Being made aware of the cloud of witnesses who surround us and their contributions to the Christian faith shape those of us who worship in that space.

The same is true in the worship space of the small membership church. All that surrounds us in that room says something about who we are. An important educational task is to help people know about and understand the various images and symbols, why they are in the worship space, and what they represent and say about the people who have worshiped there in the past and are worshiping there now. This can be done through intentional teaching moments when the pastor or a church leader talks about the symbols. It can be done through the church bulletin where each week a different symbol is highlighted. Such teaching about the worship space can't be a one-time-only proposition. It needs to be an ongoing process. Learning about our worship space is important Christian education in the small membership church.

A second opportunity is the liturgy, or the order and form of worship. The way we worship is teaching us too. As David Ray says, "Many people participate in worship without a clear understanding of what worship is."[3] Being intentional about helping them understand is important educational work. Recognizing that the bulletin is not just a guide to worship but a teaching tool is a start.

The bulletin can contain information about a ritual. For example, we not only offer directions for how Communion is taken (helpful information for any visitor) but also offer a few words about Christ being the host of this commemorative meal and how Jesus welcomes everyone. We can offer a brief word of explanation about the call to worship and help remind people that we aren't calling God to worship—God is already here—but we are calling ourselves. We are preparing and opening ourselves to God's presence. A brief paragraph about a particular hymn, its writer and background on why it was written, offers another teachable moment. Printing questions that encourage the congregation's continued reflection on the sermon during the coming week is another example of how a bulletin can teach. When we begin to see it as a teaching tool, the possibilities for its use in our particular worship setting become obvious.

We are also teaching through the litanies we use, the prayers we pray, and the hymns we sing. I have often said to my students in seminary that one of the most important educational decisions they will make each week is the selection of hymns. We learn much of our theology through the hymns we sing, and careful thought needs to go into their choosing.

A third educational opportunity in worship is the reading of scripture and the sermon. Of course, these are probably the most obvious to most of us. But reminding ourselves of this invites us to pay attention to the teaching opportunities in these moments in worship. The reading of scripture can be done in ways that help it come alive, that challenge and stimulate our brains to listen. Using different voices for different parts of the text, organizing a brief dramatic presentation, beginning the scripture reading with some brief background on the text, its author, and its context—all of these take seriously the need to help people enter the story, connect it with their own, and make meaning for their own lives. The same is true of the sermon. Pastors are encouraged to think about different forms of delivery, to be aware that sermons are designed not only to inspire but also to teach, and to realize that the sermon moment is an important responsibility in the work of a pastor/teacher.

A final opportunity to take seriously the educational possibilities in worship is the active involvement of the people in the pews in the worship experience. Worship is not meant to be a spectator sport. Worship is the work of the people, and we all need to be active participants in it. Providing opportunities for movement, speaking aloud, singing, and praying is an important part of designing worship. Remember, the brain learns better when we are active.

Making sure every person, including children and youth, has some role in this central act of the church is vital. This can range from the preparation of flowers for the altar, the baking of communion bread, and the cleaning of the sanctuary to greeting people at the door, handing out bulletins, lighting candles, reading Scripture, offering prayers, serving Communion, and taking the offering. Lively worship with active participation by all is an important setting for education in the church!

Worship is a vital context for education in the small membership church. David Ray says it well:

> If the church teaches in everything it does and if worship is the primary time when a small church gathers, then the wise worship planner will carefully plan how that precious hour or so can be used to make and feed disciples of all ages—from the first musical note to the last. . . . The foolish pastor who only thinks about the sermon's potential to teach and inspire is wasting two-thirds of the people's time.[4]

It is important to make the best use of our educational time in the small membership church and ensure that worship is filled with promise and possibilities for the ongoing formation and nurture of disciples of Jesus.

Events

Calendars shape our lives. They note the seasons and significant moments in the year. They reflect the rhythms of our days, weeks, and months. The school calendar has shaped my own life for many years, and there is a particular rhythm that marks September through May. The liturgical calendar shapes the life of many churches. We see it reflected in the scripture texts used and the changing colors of the altar cloths and clergy stoles. The wider social calendar frames our lives through national holidays like July 4, sporting events like the Super Bowl, and local community events like Patriots' Day in Boston. As human beings, we draw a sense of identity from these events.[5] They help to tell us who we are and what we are about in the world.

Calendars shape the life of a small membership church too. The church's calendar reflects those events, those moments and seasons, that are important in the life of that community of faith. These events implicitly say something about who we are and what we are doing in the world. They also help shape the identities of those who participate in them. What we need to see is that these events are important opportunities for Christian education.[6] As we participate in these shared experiences, we come to know who we are, whose we are, and how we are to live. They are another vital context for engaging in educational ministry in the small membership church.

There are different kinds of events we experience in the life of a congregation, and each of these affords opportunity for education. There are what I call the "core events" of the church year. There are events that are a part of a particular congregation's life and history. There are events that mark personal transitions. And there are events involving the wider community.

Core events are those represented in the liturgical calendar and embodying the story of the Christian faith. These events include Advent, Christmas, Epiphany, Lent, Easter, and Pentecost. Because they occur each year, they offer structure to a congregation's life and provide shape to our educational work. Worship and Sunday school during these times draw on the biblical texts and themes appropriate to that part of the story. In worship, the symbols we use, the scriptures we read, the hymns we sing all reflect the meaning of the season. Being intentional about making people aware of this is key to educating. If a congregation holds an Advent workshop to decorate the church, thought is given to ways in which the participants will be made aware of why we do this, how this represents the Advent theme of waiting and preparation. Selecting a mission project during Lent and finding ways to make people aware of Lent's call to sacrifice and a giving of self is another example of being intentional. Core events offer many opportunities for nurturing faith and forming people in their Christian identity.

Events unique to a congregation's life and history are another context for education. The annual homecoming, Harvest

Sunday, the anniversary of the church, the yearly pancake and sausage supper—by whatever name they go, there are traditional events in each congregation's life that are important parts of that congregation's identity. They also are important moments of education. These events say something about who we are. They may say we are a family, a people of the land and stewards of God's gifts, a people of tradition, or a people of hospitality. Thinking about what each of these events says about being a Christian and being intentional about helping people be aware of this is important educational work.

Life is full of transitions. In helping people to develop across their life's journey, the church can play an important role in noting these transitional events and helping people to make meaning of them. The list of transitions is endless. A birthday, a graduation, a retirement, a marriage, the birth of a child, baptism, a driver's license, a new job—all are examples of transitions that the church can both celebrate and recognize as important moments of learning. I knew a church that celebrated everyone's birthday with an annual birthday party. People sat at tables organized around months of the year. (In a small church, it could be seasons of the year, like fall birthdays and so on.) Old and young talked about their lives and what the past year had been like. They reflected together on what a gift from God life was and sought to take seriously the psalmist's call to "teach us to number our days that we may get a heart of wisdom" (Ps 90:12 RSV). The small membership church can develop creative educational moments around the personal events in its members' lives.

Finally, there are events that involve the church in the wider community. Bazaars, community worship services, CROP walks, Habitat for Humanity projects, even those suppers we've already mentioned—are events that involve the congregation with the world outside its walls. Educationally, it is important that the church help the participants from the congregation see not only that these are social events, fund-raisers, or mission and service activities but also that they are moments when we are learning and expressing what it means to be a Christian. Providing times to reflect on these events and what they mean is vital.

Core events, unique congregational events, transitional events, and wider community events are all places in the life of the small membership church where education is happening, whether we realize it or not. Taking advantage of these natural gatherings and groupings, we can be more intentional about these contexts as places of education. First, we can make note of all the events that are central in the life of our congregation. Which core events do we highlight? What are our unique congregational events? What personal transitions seem especially important in the lives of these folks? In what community events do we participate?

Second, we can provide instruction about these events. We can teach people both formally and informally the biblical stories and texts that offer theological meaning to these experiences. For example, we can gather those preparing the annual sausage supper for a time of devotion where we reflect on biblical images of hospitality and welcome. Or before the annual homecoming, we can plan a Sunday worship service devoted to the theme of what it means to be the family of God.

And finally, we can take the time after the events to reflect on them and to assess what happened. Asking ourselves how this event helped to nurture Christian discipleship is a critical question. Gathering a small representative group to do this is useful. It doesn't have to take a great deal of time, but any time spent in this kind of intentional assessment and evaluation is time well spent and provides helpful information for the task of educating people in their faith.

Seeing events as contexts for education in the church provides some meaningful benefits to the small membership church. Such events naturally lend themselves to intergenerational involvement. We don't have to plan separate intergenerational opportunities but can use the ones already present in our midst. Events offer what I call *embodied* education. We learn by participating and doing. It is active learning that involves the whole person, the best way for learning to occur! And events provide natural opportunities for evangelism, for sharing the good news with those around us. As friends and neighbors sit around tables at the annual sausage supper, it is often easier to talk about why you are doing this. People also see you living your Christian beliefs, and some will want to know more.

Summary

The where and when of Christian education in the small membership church are—everywhere and all the time! Recognizing this allows us to see we don't have to create special places and special times but can utilize the ongoing life of the congregation as the context for educational ministry. Sunday school is one of those places that exist in the lives of most congregations, and we don't have to be discouraged in the small church because we don't have enough numbers or enough space. When we draw on the images of the one-room school and homeschooling, we see the possibilities for teaching and learning through a Sunday school that fits our circumstances.

But our educational space is not limited to Sunday school. Worship is a vital educational context in the small membership church. Paying attention to all the ways we are educating and can educate in that context is at the heart of educational ministry in such churches. Giving attention to space, the order and form of the service, and the active involvement of the people is key.

And finally, the events that happen regularly in the life of the congregation are natural settings for Christian education. The core events of the church year, events unique to a particular church, events that mark the transitions of life, and events that connect us to the wider community are all contexts for teaching and learning. Being mindful and intentional about all of these educational contexts offers many possibilities for exciting and creative educational ministry in the small membership church.

Further Reflection

1. What is your church currently doing with Sunday school? What did the concepts of a one-room school and homeschooling

help you see about doing Christian education in your setting? Who might help you think further about these images for your church? What next steps can you take?

2. Think about your current worship service.

- What is in the worship space? How are people made aware of this space and what all that is in it means and represents? What more could be done?
- How is your current worship bulletin being used to educate people? What are some new ways it could be used?
- What could be done to enhance the educational nature of the worship service? What steps need to be taken to help this happen?

3. Make a list of all the events you can name that are a part of your congregation's life. Organize these according to whether they are core events, unique events, transition events, or community-wide events. (Some may belong in more than one category.)

- Which category of events is the strongest, has the most participation? Why do you think that is so?
- Which category of events has the fewest participants? Why do you think that is so?
- What events could be added? What events are no longer helpful and need to be ended?

4. Pick an event important in the life of the congregation.

- In what ways are you currently educating through this event?
- What might be done to enhance the teaching and learning?
- What steps need to be taken to help this happen?

4

How: Clues to Education in the Small Membership Church

M any students have passed through the doorways of my classrooms across the years. I have learned that foremost in their minds is the question "How do I do it?" How do I do Christian education in the local church? It is an important question. The challenge comes in the answer they often expect. They expect me to offer them a step-by-step guaranteed process for doing education. And my challenge is to help them see that carrying out educational ministry in the church cannot be reduced to a step-by-step process and that there are no guarantees!

Like I said earlier in this book, how we do education depends on many factors. One of the most important steps in doing Christian education is learning to think carefully and critically about it and to consider some of the issues we've already addressed, issues like what our concept of education is, who the people we educate are, and where does education occur and how does that shape what we do. Thinking and reflecting on these issues is actually a part of the how of Christian education. So we've already been talking about how!

Having said that, there are some additional clues related to how we do it that are important to discuss. These include the process and methods we use, two important capacities we need to engage, and the role of story and ritual in education.

Process and Methods

Process refers to the broad approach we use in educating. It provides an outline of how we proceed. *Model* is another term I've heard used to talk about the approach that guides our organizing and structuring of education.[1] *Methods* refers to those specific activities and techniques we use within a process or model to help people learn. Methods include things like lectures, discussions, small group activities, role-playing, drama, singing, and so on.[2]

In many of the churches I've known, no single model exists in pure form. We utilize aspects of various models to put together an approach to Christian education that works for us. What is important here is to be thoughtful about what we are doing and seek to name our approach, to say what we are doing in order that we might, with intentionality, do it better.

In the small membership church, one of the most vital approaches to Christian education is what I would call a community model. It draws on the reality that everything a church does is educating, and it seeks to integrate all aspects of the church's life in ways that consistently move people deeper into their identity as disciples of Jesus Christ. As David Ray says, "Christian education goals are best achieved by involvement with the whole community, by providing role models and mentors, and by praxis or applying what has been taught in real life experiences."[3]

What is important to me is to consider the characteristics that need to shape whatever structure we use to organize educational ministry in the small membership church. There are five vital qualities that are basic to doing Christian education in this setting. These qualities are (1) experiential, (2) reflective, (3) relational, (4) inclusive, and (5) integrative.

1. *Christian education in the small membership church needs to be experiential.* To say education needs to be experiential is to state the obvious, but often the obvious needs to be stated. The issue here is not that education is to be experiential—all life is experiential—but to give thought to the kinds of experiences we use in educational ministry. Keeping children sitting for long periods in chairs while a teacher talks on and on is not good experiential education. Having the pastor just lecture during an adult Bible study is not good experiential education. Having few opportunities for movement during the worship service is not good experiential education. Although each of the moments I mentioned could be classified as an experience, they do not involve the active engagement of the participants. We learn best when our whole selves are involved, when we see, speak, listen, move, smell, touch, and taste.

The methods we use to educate need to involve all of our senses. Whether our setting is the Sunday school, the worship service, or an event in the life of the church, we need to think about how we invite the whole person into it. For example, think about the worship service and how we invite active participation. Where can we introduce more movement? What opportunities do people have to speak? How do we learn to "taste and see that the LORD is good" (Ps 34:8)? Maybe we need to bake the Communion bread in the church on Sunday mornings so that smell, an important element in the brain's forming of memory, enriches the experience and deepens our engagement in this sacred moment. Rich and multisensory experiences are vital to Christian education in any setting, including the small membership church.

2. *Christian education in the small membership church needs to be reflective.* Experience alone isn't enough. To really learn and form those neuronal networks we talked about in an earlier chapter, we need to reflect on the experience. The brain can take in only so much material before it needs to reflect. If we want learning to occur, we need to think about it, ponder it,

discuss it, and actively process it. This too seems to be stating the obvious about education. But I've had enough experiences in the church where the emphasis was on covering the material, and getting the lesson taught with little time left to think and discuss, to realize that stating the obvious seems important. Even in worship, there are few moments to ponder, to think about what is being heard, and seldom is there opportunity to talk with others about the experience.

Reflection takes time. A minute for questions at the end of a Bible study or a moment of silence during the worship is not enough. Reflection calls for participation in various questioning activities where we think about what we've heard, what we believe about it, and what difference it makes in our lives. Questions in the worship bulletin to take home and ponder or time for discussion after worship are examples of reflective opportunities.

Reflection involves head and heart, both thinking and feeling. Our faith is not only about belief but also involves trust and compassion. We need time to reflect on our feelings as well as our thoughts. Building in opportunities for reflection on both thoughts and feelings is vital to education, whether in Sunday school, worship, or the events of congregational life. The small membership church already knows that numbers are not the most helpful measuring rods for success. So it doesn't matter how much we cover in a lesson or how long the sermon is. It is more about how well we come to know and understand what we've heard and done.

3. *Christian education in the small membership church needs to be relational.* Education is rooted in relationships. It is simply not true to claim we are self-educated. At the very least we've read books that others have written. The small membership church is rooted in relationships too. Almost everyone knows almost everyone else, and they care deeply about one another. It isn't so much that we need to make education in the small membership church relational. What we need is to be intentional about this relational quality of the church and to build on it in important ways when we organize our educational ministry.

The problem is that we tend to limit ourselves to certain kinds of relationships when we think about education. The relationship we most often associate with education is that of teacher and student, with one being the giver of information and the other the recipient. If we broaden our vision of educational relationships to see the place of mentors, role models, guides who help us find the way, companions who walk with us, friends who are there for us when we need them, and those who serve as midwives to help us bring to life new ways of living and being, then we have broadened the opportunities for education in the small membership church. We don't need classrooms with teachers. What we need is people committed to walking together in discipleship and continuing to grow and learn in all that they do as a congregation.

4. *Christian education in the small membership church needs to be inclusive.* When we think about inclusion, we think about taking everything and everyone into account, involving everyone. By its very nature, the small membership church lends itself to an inclusive Christian education. For example, we simply don't have the luxury of separate, closely age-graded classes in Sunday school. We don't have the people or resources to organize lots of separate programs focused on just one population of people. Instead, we have to think about how we include all ages together to do something. Such a perspective frees us from having to look like the larger church with its multiple classes, separate youth groups, and long list of group-specific activities.

As we've already discussed, the intergenerational nature of the small church is obvious. This nature becomes a gift that helps us think about how to include various ages in a Sunday morning church school, how to involve all ages in worship, and how to engage the various events in the life of the congregation in a way that everyone has a part. The small membership church has an abundant opportunity to model for the world the all-inclusive nature of God's love, to reflect the truth of Jesus' prayer that we are indeed all one in the eyes of God (John 17:20-21).

5. *Christian education in the small membership church needs to be integrative.* Closely related to the quality of being inclusive is the

quality of being integrative. Not only can the small membership church model an inclusive educational ministry, it can highlight the integrative nature of education. To integrate something is to bring it together, make it whole and unified. We've said it before, and we need to say it again: everything the church does is teaching, educating in what it means to be a disciple of Jesus Christ.

The small membership church needs to recognize that everything we do is educating and become intentional in working toward a holistic approach to its educational ministry. Planning church school, worship, and the various congregational events should be seen not as activities separate from one another but rather as all being a part of the educational work of the church. A church doesn't need a long and involved planning process to do this. Most small churches don't like long-range planning and lots of committees or meetings, preferring instead a more informal approach. But learning to ask how whatever is happening is helping people form Christian identity is key to an integrative approach to Christian education in the small membership church.

Although none of the five qualities discussed are particularly exclusive to education in the small membership church, they are nonetheless vital to how we do education in that setting. Taking seriously the rich experiences that form our lives, being reflective about these experiences so we learn from them, building on the natural emphasis on relationships in the small church setting, drawing on the intergenerational nature of our context, and recognizing education as integrated within the whole life of the church are all a part of how we do education in the small church.

Imagine and Improvise

There are two vital capacities we have as human beings that can be of great help in doing Christian education in the small membership church. These capacities are key to learning and to creativity. They are present in all of us, simply there for the asking. In order to carry out creative and vital education in any setting, these capacities need to be engaged. Part of the work in learning how to do education in the small membership church is recognizing, nurturing, and using these capacities. They provide vision and energy to see all the opportunities and possibilities for educating present in the small church context. These capacities are imagination and improvisation.

Imagination

One of the gifts Jesus had was the gift to imagine a different world. He could actually see a world where each one knew himself or herself themselves as a loved child of God, where the hungry were fed, the naked were clothed, the captives were freed, the blind could see, and all were welcome. Because he could imagine it, it was a possibility that he committed his life and ministry to bringing about, and countless people since have also committed themselves to such a vision. I often think our problem in the church is one of imagination and will. We don't allow ourselves to imagine the possibilities and then lack the will to help what we imagine become reality. This isn't a naive belief that anything is possible. Instead, it is the firm conviction that more is possible than we ever let ourselves realize!

One of the vital tools for doing education in the small membership church is imagination. Our brains have the amazing capacity to form something in our minds that is not yet real or present. As the Bible says it, we can see visions (Joel 2:28; Acts 2:17). Learning to utilize imagination on a regular basis in the planning, organizing, and carrying out of educational ministry in the small membership church is basic to the effectiveness of this ministry.

How can this be done? Learning to think beyond "We've always done it this way" is one way. When we hear that phrase or some variation of it, we can name the way we've always done it and then think about one thing we might do new this time. Too much change all at once can lead people across the challenge/threat line in their brains, and, when threatened, we tend to become even more rigid. But one small variation in the routine can be exciting and wake up those brains that have become less alert because of routine. After a while, it will feel more natural to explore some alternatives. For example, small changes in the order of worship can enliven that setting and make it more educationally alive.

Another way is to move beyond negative thinking to focus on what is possible. Too often in the small membership church, we focus on what we don't have or what we can't do. Instead, talk about what is possible. Brainstorming is a great tool here. For example, when thinking about whether to hold a vacation Bible school, brainstorm all of the ways in which your church might do this. Nothing is too ridiculous or silly or beyond the scope to name. Once a list has been generated, then you can go back and weed out what really isn't doable. But you can miss something if you do this too soon. Let your imaginations roam freely at the start.

Invite as many people as possible to help you imagine. New eyes can see things that familiar eyes miss. Familiarity breeds poor vision. Many times we are so familiar with something that we see only what we already know instead of coming to know what is really before us.

Welcome curiosity and questions. Children and youth are often helpful guides here. They are curious about the world and ask questions others won't. Too often we think education is about answers when it is the questions that are critical. Without the right questions, we can never come to the right answers. Learning to ask questions and explore possibilities engages the imagination and helps us see, learn, and discover new ways.

Finding ways to nurture and use imagination in our educational work in the church is important. This wonderful human capacity will help us see in new ways and can bring vitality and life to how we do Christian education in the small membership church.

Improvisation

Not only was Jesus gifted at imagination, he was a great improviser too. Using what was at hand was a hallmark of his teaching style. Whether it was some seeds being sown, common elements like salt and leaven, or some simple loaves and fishes, he drew his teaching tools from what was around him. The same was true of the settings of his teaching. He used synagogues, wells, mountains, homes, boats, fields, walks, and banquets as places to teach. Rather than thinking about what he didn't have, he improvised!

Improvisation is the capacity to act and to create in the moment in response to what is in one's immediate environment. It is often used in theater circles to help actors develop skill in being able to respond to whatever is happening onstage at any given moment. It can be very useful in the small membership church to help us take what we have and create educational ministry out of that, rather than worrying about what we don't have and getting stuck in our complaints.

Improvisation calls for attention to the moment and what is going on now. It asks that we take inventory of who we are, what we have, and think about the possibilities present in all of this. Maybe we don't have all the classroom space we want, but we can do something with the space we have. We can improvise. I've seen this done in small churches that decide to use the Workshop Rotation Model for their Sunday schools.[4] One of the often used workshops is a theater workshop, and large churches will design rooms with theater seats, a large screen, and a popcorn machine. A small church seldom has the resources to create space like that. Improvisation invites us to see that the TV and VCR or DVD player we already have and the microwave in the kitchen will work just as well, and a theater workshop in the small membership church is born.

As you can see, improvisation and imagination go hand in hand. Improvisation calls us to take what we have and do something with it. Imagination helps us see what we have that we might have overlooked. Nurturing both of these capacities contributes in important ways to the educational ministry of the small membership church.

Story and Ritual

A final clue for doing Christian education in the small membership church is the use of story and ritual. "History is the strength of the small church."[5] Such churches cherish their past. And stories are the way they share this history. Small membership churches are places of story, and there are important stories to tell. Helping the church tell its stories and link those stories to the larger biblical story that shapes and forms our identity as Christians is a vital part of Christian education. How do we do Christian education in the small membership church? We tell stories.

Stories help us discover and define who we are. Stories help us belong. Stories help us celebrate. Stories give us hope. Stories can energize us and provide a vision for the future. Throughout the church's life—in Sunday school, in worship, during events, in informal fellowship times—there are opportunities to tell and reflect on stories.

The key here is the linking of stories. Anne Streaty Wimberly introduces the concept of story linking in her writing.[6] To her the process of story linking is building connections between our personal, everyday stories; our heritage stories, both church and cultural; and the Christian faith story in the Bible in order that we might live more faithfully in the world. It isn't just the stories of the Bible that we tell in church. We also tell our personal stories, our churches' stories, and our wider heritage stories. We link all of these stories together to help us make meaning for our lives. Story linking is a natural learning process for our brains. With its innate drive to connect and form neuronal networks, using stories to teach is a very brain-friendly approach.

There are simple ways to tell stories. Asking people to share a favorite memory of childhood is inviting them to begin to tell their story. Remember, you need to provide a safe space for such storytelling. People need to know their stories will be heard with grace and love.[7] Including a story about a founding father or mother of the congregation in the church's newsletter is a way to share a heritage story. Celebrating the anniversary of the founding of the church each year is a storytelling process. Dramatizing a biblical story in the worship service rather than just reading it is an enriched form of storytelling. Using our capacity to imagine, we can discover all the ways in which stories already are told and new ways they can be told and reflected upon within the lives of our congregation.

Rituals are an important part of this storied process too. Rituals are patterned, shared behaviors that provide order and shape to our world. The way we begin our church school class, the prayer said before a meal, the order of worship we use, the way we pray in church, the devotional that begins a committee meeting—all of these are examples of rituals in the life of the church. As David Hogue reminds us, "Our rituals are rehearsals of the stories that define us."[8]

Take Communion as an example. We aren't just eating a small piece of bread and taking a sip of wine or grape juice in this sacrament of the church. We are rehearsing a story, a story of welcome, of love, of inclusion, of room at the table for everyone. As we enact, or tell, that story each time we share Communion, we are living our faith and forming ourselves ever more deeply in our identity as Christians. Helping people see the stories represented in our rituals is a vital educational task.

Educationally, it is very important to think about the rituals of our congregation. What are the patterned and shared regular behaviors that order our lives? What do we do in worship and how is that shaping us? Do we want to be shaped in that way? How do we begin meetings in our church? How does this reflect the faith story we claim? All of these are important educational questions. The rituals we engage are shaping us. They are rehearsing the stories that define us. We need to be sure that the shape and definition reflect the gospel we claim!

Summary

There isn't one right way to do Christian education in the small membership church. However we do it, though, it needs to be experiential, reflective, relational, inclusive, and integrative. The experiences we provide need to be rich and complex, including active participation and the use of a variety of senses. The need for reflection reminds us to provide time to think and ponder. The emphasis on relationships encourages us to see that people are at the heart of all we do and that we need not limit ourselves to one kind of relationship in education. The call to inclusion helps us see the intergenerational nature of the church and to build on this gift. The challenge to be integrative reminds us that everything we do as a congregation is educating.

Education in the small membership church calls for the use of our capacities to imagine and to improvise. Imagination and improvisation are gifts that enable us to see in new ways, to envision what is not yet but might be, and to make use of whatever we have at hand in the ministry of education. We also need to see the power of story and ritual and become a story-telling people who regularly rehearse our stories throughout the life of the congregation. There are stories to tell and, through the telling, a witness to be made to the gospel that forms our congregation's life.

Further Reflection

1. Engage in a brief writing exercise:

- Write the following on a piece of paper: "My church is ..." Then start writing, putting down whatever comes into your head. Write for five minutes. Do not edit or worry about things like spelling or grammar. Just write!
- Make a list of the characteristics and qualities describing your church that are mentioned in your writing.
- Compare your list to the five qualities discussed in this chapter: experiential, reflective, relational, inclusive, and integrative. In what ways do the five qualities describe your church? In what ways is your church different?

- How are the qualities you've listed for your church influencing the way educational ministry is carried out there? How might you imagine doing it differently?

2. Practice improvisation. (This is best done with a small group of people. It can be a church group or members of your family or friends.)

- Collect four or five familiar household items like a kitchen utensil, a garden tool, a toy, a pill bottle, and so on. Be creative in choosing the items!
- Take one item at a time and pass it around. Ask each person to imagine this is an item they have never seen before and that they are to come up with a description and use for it. Each person must come up with a new use.
- When you are finished with all of the items, reflect together for a few minutes on what happened and what you learned about improvising from the exercise.

3. There are various ways to help your congregation tell its story. Here is an exercise using a congregational time line:[9]

- Post a long sheet of butcher paper on the wall. At the top, mark off the relevant years or decades for your congregation, beginning with the date it was organized. Put in the names of pastors at the appropriate points and add any other dates of significance, including public events like wars, natural calamities, civic events, and so on, that impacted congregational life.
- Invite the members present to place a symbol at the point when their presence in the congregation began.
- Take time to tell stories of their memories of the congregation and encourage them to place an appropriate symbol and a brief note on the time line to mark their story.
- At the end of the exercise, take a few minutes to review the time line and see if you can name some seasons or chapters

in the church's life. Make a list of the qualities and values that seem to have sustained the church's life.
• Close with a favorite congregational hymn and prayer.
• Leave the time line on the wall and encourage people to continue to add to it.
• This is a good exercise to do in connection with a home-coming celebration or a church anniversary.

5

Resources

My husband and I enjoy watching the PBS series *This Old House*. As we watch the crew work their magic on the chosen house, we often say to each other that you can do just about anything with enough money and the right kind of tools. But the money and right tools are not always available to the average home owner. So we learn to adapt and improvise.

The same could be said of the small membership church when it comes to resources for Christian education. We could do anything with enough money and the right kind of tools. But generally we work with limited financial means and struggle to find the right materials for our setting. So we learn to adapt and improvise.

Learning to use what is at hand is an important act of stewardship in the church. When we take a careful look at it, there is a lot at hand in terms of resources that can help us do the work of educational ministry in the small membership church. It is all in how we look at it. In this chapter, I want to help us look at three important categories of resources available to us and think about how we can make the best use of them. These resources are people, space, and curriculum materials.

People

Often when we think of resources, we think of material items like books, computers, CDs, DVDs, tables, chairs, chalkboards, and so on. We overlook the human resources and the role they play in Christian education. Rather than overlooking them, we need to see that *people are the most important resource we have.* David Ray says it well: "Faith cannot be *taught* by objective instruction. Faith is caught as one experiences it in the Christian community."[1] Our children and youth may not always be studying their Bibles and Sunday school lessons as diligently as we would like, but they are studying the lives of the people around them. Every member of the congregation is teaching about the Christian faith in all that they say and do. People are our most important resource!

Recognizing and acknowledging this is an important step in utilizing the resources we have in the small membership church. Helping people see that they are teaching through their actions and interactions with one another, both within the church and elsewhere, is an important educational task of the leadership of a church. Many churches hold some kind of homecoming or rally day in the early fall to signal the start of a new church program year. Often this is a time when teachers and leaders in Christian education are recognized and commissioned to their work. I believe it is a good time for the church members as a whole to rededicate themselves to the call we all have through baptism, to live as faithful Christians each day. In our daily living, we are teaching others what it means to claim the name of Christ.

Beyond the claim that people are our most important resource, what more needs to be said about them? We need to look at how we make use of this resource. What are some important clues for engaging people in the most helpful ways? There are three clues that are especially helpful in the small membership church. The first is to remember that teachers and leaders are called, not just recruited or drafted. The second is that we need to use a team approach. And third, everyone has gifts to share.

1. *Teachers and leaders are called.* It's time to take down the recruiting poster or leave out the notice in the church newsletter that calls for volunteers to teach and lead in the Christian education ministry. Instead, we need to follow the model of Jesus and call forth those in our midst who have the qualities we want and

need in those who teach and lead. Jesus did not wait for the disciples to volunteer. Instead, he went looking for them and called them forth into ministry. From the earliest pages of our sacred text, we see a God who calls, who asks some of the most unlikely people to step out in faith and become partners in God's creating and redeeming work in the world.

There are those in our small membership church who display a deep love and respect for others, who have a passion for the gospel and for sharing it, who love to learn and invite others to love learning too. All of these are key qualities for those who teach and lead. Once we set aside our preconceived notions of what a teacher looks and acts like (for example, one who knows it all or can lecture for thirty minutes on a subject), we see the special people in our midst who can be teachers, mentors, and guides. Spending time in prayer and seeking God's guidance is an important part of this process of calling. Asking those who are called to seek God's wisdom is key too.

It is important to remember that the whole church has an important role to play in this call. We don't invite people to teach and then leave them without support and nurture. The church needs to demonstrate that it places a priority on education by providing resources and help for the task. It shows that teachers are appreciated and needed by saying thank you in multiple ways. It doesn't expect a teacher to teach forever but asks for a specific time commitment. And it realizes that a teacher's time is precious. If the conventional Sunday school format on Sunday morning does not work in your church, you don't waste a teacher's time trying to make it happen. Instead, thought is given to doing education in other ways and helping those called to teach to use their gifts appropriately in different contexts.

2. Use a team approach. I often say to my students in seminary that ministry was never meant to be the work of a Lone Ranger. Just look again at Jesus as our model. He called the Twelve to assist him in his work. He didn't try to do it all by himself. When he sent the disciples out in ministry, he sent them out two by two (Mark 6:7). We were never meant to do this work alone!

This is especially true of Christian education in the small membership church. Drawing on the community model I mentioned earlier, we remember that we are a small group of people formed together into a community of faith, the Body of Christ. And, like the body image that Paul uses in 1 Corinthians 12:12-27, we need one another. We can't function at our best without the other parts of the body doing their part.

Everyone in the small membership church is a part of the Christian education team. The pastor doesn't do it by himself or herself. Teachers do not function in isolation from parents and grandparents. The Christian education committee doesn't do its work in isolation from the worship committee or the mission committee. Children and youth do not journey alone without adult companions. Adults benefit from the perspective of the young, remembering that "a little child shall lead them" (Isa 11:6). As we've said several times in these pages, it is the whole life of the congregation that educates. Working as a team, the small membership church recognizes that everyone is a vital resource in the ministry of Christian education.

3. *Everyone has gifts to share.* As a member of the team, everyone has a gift to share in helping to resource educational ministry. Your calling may not be as a teacher or a leader, but there are things you can contribute. Too often we look at what we can't do rather than focusing on what we can do. I've wondered what went through the mind of the little boy who found himself in the crowd listening to Jesus on that hillside long ago (John 6:1-13). When the time came to eat and the call for food went out from the disciples, he probably looked at his small lunch and thought it was too little to make a difference. Of course, we know the story—that small lunch provided the basis for the feeding of multitudes.

All of us have something to contribute to the work of education in our church. A family could take on a service project of providing art supplies for the vacation Bible school for one summer. A musician could volunteer to teach the children a new song once a month during a children's moment in worship. A carpenter could offer to build some much-needed equipment for the children's Sunday school room. In my small membership congregation, there is a young man who is a gifted artist. He has taken on the responsibility of creating attractive bulletin boards related to the various seasons of the church year. Youth can read Bible stories to the children, and older adults can share their faith stories with youth as a part of confirmation.

No gift is too small in the eyes of God. When we realize that everyone is a contributor to the educational ministry of the church, we will begin to see the possibilities present in our community of faith. No longer will we struggle to find the people we need. We will see that God has placed in our midst the people and gifts necessary for forming faithful disciples of Jesus Christ. We will celebrate the people resources we have and give thanks to God for such gifts.

Space

One of the things that is often in short supply in the small membership church is space. Sometimes in the large, urban churches that have seen their membership dwindle, there is plenty of space, but it is not configured in ways helpful to doing Christian education with small numbers. Yet space of any kind is a resource if we are able to see the possibilities in it. Our goal is space that is "alive and conducive to being, playing, studying, praying, and working together."[2]

To my thinking, space isn't so much about quantity as it is quality. "Virtually any space can be made to work with some ingenuity, scavenging and recycling, a little paint, and some spit and polish."[3] I know a church that turned an out-of-the-way corner in a hallway into an inviting reading area for children with a little paint, some simple bookshelves, and pillows on the floor. Another congregation took a single classroom and—with a wall mural designed and painted by adult and children volunteers, a small platform in one corner for dramas and role plays, a table and chairs in another corner for a craft area, and a remnant of carpet on the floor defining a worship and storytelling area—created an inviting one-room school environment for its small and multiple-aged group of children.

When we think about our space resources, we need to consider them from two perspectives. First, we need to pay attention to the physical space, its possibilities and limits, its condition, and the ways in which it facilitates our educational work. We also need to attend to what I call emotional space, the feelings and attitudes people experience in a particular environment. Both physical and emotional qualities are key aspects of space and need our attention as we work with our space resources.

Physical space

Peeling paint, crumbling plaster, broken furniture, musty smells, supplies in disarray on shelves, dust and grime everywhere—these conditions make an important statement. They say to those who enter such space that we have not prepared for your coming. We haven't given thought to your welfare or well-being. This is certainly a message I would not want to convey about the gospel of Jesus Christ! Basic cleanliness and items in good repair are the starting point when it comes to our space resources.

Whatever space we have, be it large or small, be it the sanctuary, the narthex, the fellowship hall that we divide into classroom space on Sunday morning, or the room that serves as both a library and adult study space, needs to convey a message of hospitality. It needs to say that people are wanted, expected, and welcomed here.

We say welcome in a variety of ways. We make sure there is adequate light, comfortable temperature, furniture and acoustics that fit the needs of our people. We don't ask aging bodies to sit on rickety metal folding chairs. We don't crowd children and youth into small spaces that allow little room for movement. We remember that the brain learns best when it is stimulated. "When you invite students into an environment that is rich with stimulants for the brain, learning happens. When you invite students into a sterile, dull, or rigid environment, learning is hampered."[4]

74

We take time to enrich our spaces with sights, sounds, smells, textures, and tastes that help us learn.

Providing this kind of space does not have to cost a lot of money. Nor do you need lots of space to pay attention to these details. Organize a volunteer work group to clean regularly and keep space from becoming cluttered. This is a good service project for a church with limited resources for custodial staff. You can create art for the walls from those coffee-table books they sell at used-book fairs. The pictures in these books can be cut out, mounted on simple construction paper, and laminated for use. Invite an artist in the congregation to paint a mural, like the one described earlier. Ask a carpenter to build the bookcases you need for the children's reading corner. Think creatively and you will be amazed at what can be done with limited resources to create inviting and welcoming physical space. And you will be using your people resources too!

Emotional space

Space isn't just a physical reality. It is also an emotional reality. Many of us can describe what it feels like to be in a space where we naturally feel at home. We want to sit down, prop up our feet, and stay awhile. We can also describe space where we don't feel safe, even when there is no evidence of physical threat.

When we don't feel welcome, when we are afraid to say what we believe and feel, when we feel threatened by those who seem to hold the power in a situation, we have a difficult time being open to learning. Our energy is spent trying to protect ourselves. We've crossed that challenge/threat line in our brains and have a limited capacity to learn.

It saddens me to say that this kind of emotional environment can be found in the church. There are congregations in which people do not feel welcome, even small membership congregations where relationships are supposed to be at the heart of congregational life. Seldom are people told they aren't wanted, but nothing is done to include them. People are afraid to express their opinions in a Bible study for fear that they will be ridiculed, put down, or rejected by others. The rejection doesn't have to be obvious but can be as subtle as a roll of the eyes or a deep sigh that says, "Boy, that's stupid."

What helps create positive emotional space? Hospitality, openness, and a sense of safety are key. Hospitality is the act of welcoming another. We receive them with warmth and care. We attend to their physical needs. We help people feel at home. Not only do we welcome people but we also welcome ideas and perspectives that may be different from our own, but from which we can learn. In hospitable space, the welcome mat is out for both people and ideas, saying please come in, sit awhile, and let us learn from one another.

Openness refers to a sense of freedom and invitation to be ourselves. In open space, people feel free to share what they are thinking and feeling, to ask questions, and to deal with hard issues without fearing attack or ridicule. We are free to disagree, knowing that in our differences there are opportunities to learn.

Ironically, boundaries are important to open space. Space without limits is chaotic, and it is difficult to learn in chaos. Boundaries provide a sense of security, letting us know what we can count on in this space. They provide a sense of safety, the third factor that helps create positive emotional space.

I've mentioned before about the role fear plays in hindering the brain's ability to learn. People need to feel safe if you want them to learn. An obvious boundary, of course, is that physical violence will not be tolerated. People don't feel safe if they are worried about their physical well-being. But keeping physical violence out of our churches isn't enough. There are other kinds of violence that do damage to people and prevent the kind of open exchange in which education can thrive.

When we make fun of people or allow others to make them the target of a joke, when we respond with sarcasm, ridicule, and put-downs, we are perpetuating violence upon another. The old adage "Sticks and stones may break my bones, but words can never hurt me" is simply not true. Words are among the most powerful weapons we unleash on one another. The damage can have long-term effect. Allowing children, youth, or adults to call one another stupid or to use other terms of ridicule is an example of such violence. Free of violence, positive emotional space is shaped by grace, love, and care.

Don't assume because almost everyone knows one another in the small membership church that we don't have to pay attention to hospitality, openness, and safety. Sometimes we can be the rudest to our own families and forget about the simple social graces that smooth the way and create hospitable and open space. Or we overlook them and forget to say thank you for all they do. Sometimes we assume that, because we are members of the same family, we all think the same and we squelch differences of opinion. Hospitality, openness, and safety are important qualities for learning space wherever we are.

Curriculum Materials

"The curriculum you choose is less important than the environment and the teachers and mentors you provide."[5] With these words, David Ray speaks important wisdom for us to hear. Curriculum materials don't teach; people do! Space teaches too, which is why we have to pay attention to it. But that being said, curriculum materials are helpful tools, and learning how to find and select good ones for the small membership church is important.

It would be convenient if I could now list the best possible resource for the small membership church to use. But I can't! There are multiple resources available, and their usefulness depends on the particularities of a given church. We need to get over the myth that we can find just the right resource that will solve our problems and do our educational work for us. It's become a stewardship issue for me. Churches spend money continually buying the latest resource that supposedly holds the magic formula for success. It doesn't work quite the way they thought it would, and they buy new materials while the old resources collect dust in the supply closet. Because of limited financial means, small membership churches sometimes just give up and make do with whatever they can find. Neither approach is helpful in selecting curriculum materials.

There are some intentional and deliberate steps we can take that help us think through our needs, review the resources out there, and make good use of them. The process begins with description. Like a good physician making a diagnosis, we don't begin by writing the prescription, that is, selecting the resource. We begin with describing who we are and what is needed. We take time to think about our congregation and what we want in the materials we choose. In appendix 2, you will find a self-evaluation questionnaire that can help you in this process.

A part of this description process involves the curriculum materials themselves. We don't select materials without first looking them over and spending some time evaluating them for our purposes. Get samples of the materials you are considering and spend some time reviewing them.[6] In appendix 3, you will find a curriculum materials evaluation checklist that can assist in this.

It is important to make this descriptive process a team effort. Pastor, teachers, parents, representatives of the students themselves, and leaders of the congregation all need a voice in selecting materials. If we truly believe that Christian education is the whole church's responsibility, then the whole church needs to have a stake in selecting the materials we will use to educate.

The process I've described and the checklists I've provided are especially useful in selecting materials to be used in church school settings. But, as we discussed earlier, there are multiple contexts within which the small membership church educates, including worship and intergenerational events. We need resources for these contexts too. To guide you in finding materials for your particular setting, I've provided a bibliography in appendix 4. It is not an exhaustive bibliography, but it will get you started. It includes suggested Sunday school resources, materials for intergenerational use, websites, and books on the small membership church that include useful material on education and worship.

There is one additional resource that you will find in appendix 5. This is a bibliography of children's literature.[7] We talked about the importance and power of story in chapter 4. Children's stories are a valuable resource for education in the small membership church. And their use is not limited to children. I have seen the power of a well-chosen children's story at work during the children's moment in worship (adults are listening too!), with youth as they spend time reading to children, and with adults at a committee meeting as they experience an opening devotion built around a children's story. I encourage you to explore the use of children's literature as a curriculum resource in your small membership church. Begin to develop a small library of children's literature. You can utilize your people resources by holding a book shower, where people are invited to purchase and give to the church one of the books on the bibliography.

So we've evaluated and finally purchased our resources. But the process doesn't end there. We don't just hand people materials and tell them to go use them. We need to help them learn how to use the resources. We can schedule a workshop, either as an individual church or in cooperation with others, on the use of materials. We can invite those with experience to be mentors with new teachers. We realize that being good stewards of what we have is making sure it is put to good use!

The final step in our process of finding and using curriculum materials is evaluation. Evaluation occurs any time we ask the question "How are things working?" We don't wait to do this until there are problems. On an ongoing basis, we check to see how things are working. Informal conversations, observations, discussions with teachers, parents, children, and youth—all of these can help us evaluate what is happening. The process of selecting curriculum materials includes the ongoing evaluation of their use.

Summary

Resources for doing Christian education in the small membership church abound if we but learn how to see them. The most important resource we have is our people. They teach with their daily lives, and our work is to help people see and understand this. We need to follow in the footsteps of Jesus and call forth those in our midst who are meant to be our teachers. But it is not only teachers who are called. All of us are called to be a part of the educational team that is the small membership church. We are to share the gifts we have, knowing that even the smallest gesture can make a difference.

Seeing space as a resource and not a problem is important to our educational work. It isn't the quantity of space we have but what we do with what we have that matters. Taking care of the physical setting, making sure it is clean, vibrant and alive, and filled with multiple stimulation to excite minds and hearts is a vital task. Paying attention to the emotional atmosphere of our context is a necessary part of learning too. A hospitable, open, and safe space provides an environment conducive to learning and growing as disciples of Jesus Christ.

Finally, curriculum resources are a necessary tool for educating in the small membership church. Taking time to carefully evaluate and select them is vital to finding the right materials for our unique context. But our work doesn't end once we've selected the materials. We also have to help people know how to use them and keep checking to see how they are working. People, space, and thoughtfully selected materials—these are the key resources for Christian education in the small membership church.

Further Reflection

1. How do you currently find the teachers and leaders you need for Christian education? What have you learned in this chapter that helps you rethink this? What new steps will you take to find and nurture teachers and leaders in your congregation?

2. Make a list of all the ways people have contributed to the Christian education ministry of your congregation in the past year.

- Design a worship service in which you celebrate these gifts and give thanks for them.
- Provide opportunity during the worship experience for people to reflect on a gift they might have to share and to offer that gift in service to the church.

3. Gather a group of people committed to Christian education in your church and take a walking tour of the building and grounds.

- Look at the physical conditions. Where is there need for cleanliness and repair? Who will be responsible for this?
- In what ways does your space reflect hospitality, openness, and safety? What could be done to enhance these qualities even more?
- What new possibilities for education do you now see in this space that you did not see before? In what ways could the space be made more vibrant and stimulating for learning? Who are the people in your congregation who can help make this happen?

4. Complete the questionnaire found in appendix 2.

- Select some curriculum materials already being used by your church. Reflect on how well these materials meet the criteria you named on the questionnaire. What do you discover through this exercise?
- Using the curriculum materials evaluation checklist in appendix 3, evaluate the materials you selected. What do you see about these materials that you did not notice before? How would you now rank these materials?

5. Take time to explore some of the resources listed in the bibliography in appendix 4. What did you discover? What new resource for your church did you find?

6

Guiding Principles

Our journey through some of the nuts and bolts of Christian education in the small membership church is drawing to a close. We've taken the lay of the land, thinking about some of the identifying marks of the small membership church and about the essential nature of education. We've talked about the importance of knowing our people and what they bring to the educational task. We've widened our understanding of the various contexts within which education occurs. We've considered some important how-to's for doing Christian education in the small church context. And we've looked at the multitude of resources available to us.

Through all of this, I hope one important caveat has come through loud and clear. There is no one right way to do Christian education in the small membership church. If we want to be successful in our task, we need to be intentional and deliberate, to think carefully and critically about the issues we've raised here, and to develop an educational ministry that fits our particular church and context. To guide our thinking, our dreaming, our planning, and our doing of this important ministry, we need some basic principles that will help direct our path. Drawing on the work we've done in these pages, what are some vital insights we need to keep before us as we educate in the small membership church? Although certainly not an exhaustive list, with a nod to David Letterman, let me name my top ten.

1. *Small is beautiful!* In a culture that seems to measure every-thing by size and has declared that bigger is better, it is hard to see the value in something small. "Small is typically judged as rel-ative to something else. Small does not stand on its own: it's not something of value in itself. In the language of our culture, large has more positive connotations, and small, more negative ones. To be small carries inherent limitation."[1] By definition, then, the small church is seen as deficient.

Such a perspective feeds the low morale and lack of self-esteem I've seen in small membership churches. Low morale and self-esteem contribute to a sense of defeat, that we can't really do any-thing as a church. I hear this when someone says, "Oh, we can't have Christian education in our church because we only have three children." We give up before we've even started!

It is time to declare that small is beautiful! Our sacred texts certainly claim this. Listen to them: "A little child shall lead them" (Isa 11:6); "Where two or three are gathered in my name, I am there among them" (Matt 18:20); "You must not be partial in judging: hear out the small and the great alike" (Deut 1:17); "The least among all of you is the greatest" (Luke 9:48b); and "How great a forest is set ablaze by a small fire!" (James 3:5b).

Our small size is to be celebrated and cherished for the gifts it brings. We aren't just a little church, or we don't just have forty in worship on Sunday. We are a cell in the Body of Christ and can faithfully educate our members to do and live as God would have us. Small is beautiful. Thanks be to God!

2. *Small is different.* Remember what we noted earlier: "Small churches are not smaller versions of large churches. They are qualitatively, as well as quantitatively, different."[2] One of the guiding principles for doing Christian education in the small membership church needs to be that such churches are different. We cannot use the large church as our model. Nor should becom-ing a large church necessarily be our goal. Instead, we need to see the possibilities in our smallness and develop education that fits our needs and contexts. Hopefully, the preceding chapters have helped you envision the possibilities and promise in the small church setting.

Not only is the small membership church in general different, but each church in this category is different and unique from the others. So we have to be careful to not try to fit ourselves into some mold that we think represents the small church. Our work is to know and understand our particular small church and, working as a team with others in the church, to think through together what will work and what won't in our educational ministry. Always our goal is the formation of authentic disciples of Jesus Christ, people who live their faith throughout their daily lives.

3. *Education is essential.* Walter Brueggemann once said, "Every community that wants to last beyond a single generation must concern itself with education."[3] In other words, we are one generation away from extinction in the church if we aren't educating. Whatever our size, education is essential in the community of faith.

The importance of education for the church is seen even in the earliest days of its existence. There is a story told in Acts 8:26-40 about Philip, a newly appointed apostle of the church. He encounters an Ethiopian eunuch on the road between Jerusalem and Gaza. He finds the eunuch reading the prophet Isaiah and asks him if he understands what he is reading. The eunuch's reply, "How can I, unless someone guides me?" (v. 31), sums up for me the vital necessity to be educating in the church. How can we understand what it means to be a Christian and to follow Christ unless there is guidance and nurture, unless there is education?

Thomas Groome says it well: "I will avoid claiming that education is the most important ministry in the Christian community. But I do claim that it is second to none."[4] Time, energy, and resources need to be given to this vital ministry. Our commitment is clear: education is essential to the life and vitality of the small membership church. We need to get on with the task.

4. *The whole church educates.* Even when we live by the principle that education is essential, it is still easy to relegate responsibility to certain people and to think in terms of certain structures like Sunday school. But the reality of it is that the whole church educates. It isn't just teachers working in classrooms who are

educating. The total life of the community of faith, life lived both within the walls of the church and outside the church boundaries, is teaching what it means to be a disciple of Jesus Christ.

Taking this principle seriously invites us to look at the ways our church is currently educating, both explicitly and implicitly, through its words, deeds, and behaviors. It invites us to raise important questions: What are we teaching through our life as a people? Do our words, deeds, and behaviors match? Are they reflective of the gospel? How are we helping the congregation claim its responsibility for education? Not only does it take a whole village to raise a child, it takes a whole church to educate Christian disciples.

5. *It's all about people.* We've already talked about this in chapter 2 and again in chapter 5, but it bears repeating. People are central to this important ministry of education in the church. Understanding who they are, how they learn, what it means to claim they are created in the image of God, and celebrating the resources they bring are all at the heart of Christian education in the small membership church. This attention to people seems to reflect the very nature of God. In the stories of creation as told in Genesis 1 and 2, creation was not complete without people. And the rest of the Bible seems to be a story about God's ongoing desire to be in loving relationship with people.

When we live by the principle that it is all about people, we will recognize that people are our most important resource in the small membership church. It is people who teach, who guide, who mentor, who share their gifts and talents, who gather to learn, and who model the Christian way in their everyday lives. When we live by this principle, we will see that it isn't a matter of how many children or youth we have. What counts is the attention we pay to the people we do have and the recognition that they too are children of God in need of guidance and nurture on their faith journeys. In the small membership church, we know that it is truly all about people!

6. *Use what you have.* "What do you do when there's only a few? Use the family and community structures that already exist. Toss aside concern about numbers. Plan for faithful ministry with

a few."[5] With these words, Myrtle Felkner reminds us to use what we have. Too often the small membership church lives by the mantra of "if only ..." If only we had more children or youth, if only we had more money, if only we had a bigger building, if only we could be like the bigger church down the street—the list could go on and on. We waste time on the "if onlys" that could be better focused on what we do have.

The gift this principle brings to the small membership church is the gift of seeing what we have. Too often the resources we already have are hidden from view because we are focusing so much on what we don't have. But I firmly believe that God provides the gifts and graces a community of faith needs in order to be faithful in its call to educate. We have these resources if we learn to see them. It is really a matter of learning to see in new ways. To use what we have, we have to see what we have. So start looking—you will be surprised at what you find!

7. *Imagine and improvise.* I was talking to a group of seminary students about Christian education in the small membership church. These students were already serving, in a part-time capacity, in such churches. I asked them to name the keys to doing education in such settings. One student responded, "Innovate, avoid ruts, adapt, and keep it interesting." That's what the principle of imagine and improvise is all about.

Using the human mind's wonderful ability to imagine helps us see what we haven't seen before. This opens the opportunity for innovation, for doing things in ways we hadn't tried before, for seeing resources we hadn't yet noticed. Innovation helps us avoid the ruts that can stagnate us. Adapting is at the heart of improvising. It helps us follow the previous principle of using what we have. And all of this will help keep our educational ministry interesting, stimulating our brains to learn. Exercising our capacity to imagine and improvise is vital for Christian education in the small membership church.

8. *There are stories to tell.* David Ray says that smaller churches are a "storied people."[6] He believes that stories are a vital way in which the small membership church communicates truth and

meaning. I agree. As we said in chapter 4, stories are one of the most important tools for teaching. Our brains are naturally drawn to narratives. Just watch how quickly you gather people's attention, young and old alike, when you say the words "once upon a time." They know a story is coming, and they are ready to listen.

Stories have always been vital in the lives of faith communities. Our Hebrew and Christian ancestors told stories to pass on truth and meaning about who they were and what kind of God they followed. When we share the Christian story as revealed through the stories in the Bible, we are making claim to this story and letting it shape who we are. When we tell the stories of our church lives, we are revealing truths about ourselves. Passing these stories on to our children and youth helps them claim these truths for themselves. When we share our personal stories, we are saying something important about who we are and whose we are. Remembering that there are stories to tell is vital to educational ministry in the small membership church.

9. *Space teaches.* One of the complaints I often hear in small membership churches is that there isn't enough space for Christian education. They are caught up in the amount of space and forget that it isn't the amount that matters nearly as much as the quality of the space they have. You don't need lots of space, but you do need to pay attention to what you have because space teaches!

Lessons are being taught and learned all the time in the church through the spaces we occupy. The condition of the church building, the cleanliness and quality of its rooms, the pictures and symbols around us, the emotional climate we create— all of these are teaching lessons about what it means to be a Christian in this place. It's the old adage that actions speak louder than words. Space speaks louder than words too. We may preach hospitality, but if our space is not welcoming, the message is lost. It is our task to pay attention to our space, to be aware of what kinds of lessons about the Christian life it is teaching, and to provide space that is reflective of the good news of Jesus Christ that we seek to share.

10. *Pray!* At the end of his book on the small church, Anthony Pappas says, "If all else fails, pray!"[7] Even though I certainly support his call to prayer, I believe we don't wait until failure is upon us to pray. Christian education in the small membership church is rooted and centered in prayer from the very beginning. Prayer reminds us of who's really in charge here. This is not just our work we are doing; it is God's work.

Our call in the church, as the letter to the Ephesians reminds us, is "to equip the saints for the work of ministry, for building up the body of Christ" (Eph 4:12). This is not our ministry, it is God's ministry. Prayer keeps us connected to the one who created us, called us, and now guides us on the journey. Praying should be our first guiding principle in all that we do.

As you work with the ideas in this book, as you take time to do some of the reflection exercises suggested, as you seek to develop and carry out educational ministry in your own small membership congregation, I encourage you to put prayer at the center. In our world, where aggressive action seems to be the answer to life, prayer may seem a somewhat passive response. But never underestimate its power. Remember that tiny band of people, anxious and afraid, gathered in a room on the eve of Pentecost, praying (see Acts 1 and 2). With a rush of power, the Spirit came, and the world has never been the same since.

Summary

There they are, ten guiding principles for Christian education in the small membership church: small is beautiful, small is different, education is essential, the whole church educates, people are key, use what you have, imagine and improvise, there are stories to tell, space teaches, and pray. Although these principles will not guarantee success, they can offer guidance for the important work of education to which the church has been called. May they offer insight for your own educational efforts as you seek to be faithful in fashioning the people of God in your small membership church.

Further Reflection

1. On a piece of paper, make a list of the ten principles for doing Christian education in the small membership church named in this chapter. (If working with a group, create handouts.)

- Rank the principles in terms of priority for your church. Which ones do you think are most important in your setting?
- What additional principles would you add to the list? Why? Where would these principles fall in your ranking?

2. Taking the principle that ranks number one on your list, consider the following:

- Name that which your church is currently doing that reflects this principle.
- What more could your church do to live by this principle? Make a list.
- From this list, pick the next thing you will do to live more fully by this principle.

  - What will it take to do this?
  - Whom do you need to help you?
  - What are the next steps you will take?
  - By when will you do this?

Postscript

A word of wisdom comes across the centuries from our ancient ancestors, the desert fathers. As the story goes, a brother was living among other brothers. He asked Abba Bessarion, "What should I do?" The old man replied, "Be silent, and do not measure yourself against the others."[1] So often in the small membership church, we are measuring ourselves against others, against the large megachurches that seem to have become the symbol of church in our culture. It is time we stop this measuring and claim our place as faithful communities of Christ in our own right.

When we do this, we will see the truth of another word of wisdom that comes from the *Tao Te Ching*:

> Be content with what you have;
> rejoice in the way things are,
> When you realize there is nothing lacking
> the whole world belongs to you.[2]

When it comes to carrying out educational ministry in the small membership church, there is nothing lacking. We have what we need if we but have the eyes to see and the ears to hear. My hope is that this book has helped us see and hear a little more clearly.

God is at work in our midst, forming and fashioning people in the divine likeness. Working as partners in this task, we can live in the truth that "small churches are the right size to be and do all that God calls a church to be and do—without apology and without excuse."[3] We cannot be too small to be faithful to God's call. We cannot be too small to carry out effective Christian education. Without apology and without excuse, may we carry out the work of Christian education in the small membership church, knowing that God is with us and the world awaits. May we be faithful to the task!

APPENDIX 1

Selected Bibliography on Models and Methods for Christian Education

Bracke, John, and Karen B. Tye. *Teaching the Bible in the Church.* St. Louis: Chalice Press, 2003.

Brown, Carolyn. *Developing Christian Education in the Smaller Church.* Nashville: Abingdon Press, 1982.

Bruce, Barbara. *Our Spiritual Brain.* Nashville: Abingdon Press, 2002.

Felkner, Myrtle. *From Faith to Faith: Growing Through Christian Education.* Nashville: Discipleship Resources, 2001.

Foster, Charles. *Educating Congregations: The Future of Christian Education.* Nashville: Abingdon Press, 1994.

Furnish, Dorothy J. *Experiencing the Bible with Children.* Nashville: Abingdon Press, 1990.

Galindo, Israel. *The Craft of Christian Teaching.* Valley Forge, Pa.: Judson Press, 1998.

Griggs, Donald L. *Teaching Today's Teachers to Teach.* Nashville: Abingdon Press, 2003.

Griggs, Donald L., and Judy McKay Walther. *Christian Education in the Small Church.* Valley Forge, Pa.: Judson Press, 1988.

Groome, Thomas. *Christian Religious Education.* San Francisco: Harper & Row, 1980.

Halverson, Delia. *New Ways to Tell the Old, Old Story: Choosing and Using Bible Stories with Children and Youth.* Nashville: Abingdon Press, 1992.

Juengst, Sara Covin. *Equipping the Saints: Teacher Training in the Church*. Louisville: Westminster John Knox Press, 1998.

LeFever, Marlene D. *Creative Teaching Methods*. Updated edition. Elgin, Ill.: David C. Cook, 1996.

MacQueen, Neil, and Melissa Armstrong-Hansche. *Workshop Rotation: A New Model for Sunday School*. Louisville: Westminster John Knox Press, 2000.

Rusbuldt, Richard E. *Basic Teacher Skills*. Valley Forge, Pa.: Judson Press, 1981.

Smith, Judy Gattis. *Joyful Teaching—Joyful Learning*. Nashville: Discipleship Resources, 1986.

———. *77 Ways to Energize Your Sunday School Class*. Nashville: Abingdon Press, 1992.

Wimberly, Anne Streaty. *Soul Stories: African American Christian Education*. Revised edition. Nashville: Abingdon Press, 2005.

Self-evaluation Questionnaire for Curriculum Selection

1. *Goal of the curriculum*
What do we want the curriculum we use to accomplish? What are we teaching?

2. *Bible translation*
Which of the following Bible translations are used in our church? (More than one may be checked.)

_____ New Revised Standard Version
_____ Revised Standard Version
_____ Good News
_____ New International Version
_____ King James Version
_____ Other (specify) _____

3. *Use of the Bible*
How do we want to present the biblical message to our students? (Check all that apply.)

_____ Systematic Bible study approach (that is, reading through the Bible in a systematic way, focusing on one book at a time, and so on)
_____ Topical study approach (choosing topics and selecting scripture to address the topic)
_____ Common lectionary approach
_____ Other (specify)

4. *Educational approach*
What educational approaches do we use and prefer? (Check all that apply.)

_____ Lecture and discussion
_____ Open discussion with teacher as facilitator
_____ Choices of teaching-learning activities that respond to different learning styles
_____ Use of storytelling
_____ Creative projects and crafts
_____ Story and a student book activity
_____ Other (specify)

5. *Session length*
How much actual teaching time do we have to use the curriculum materials?

_____ 30–45 minutes
_____ 45–60 minutes
_____ Expanded session (more than 60 minutes)
_____ Other (specify) _____

6. *Resources needed*
A curriculum choice usually assumes that several coordinated pieces will be purchased and used. What resources do we feel are essential to have?

_____ Teacher's guide
_____ Student book

_____ Student workbook
_____ Reproducible sheets for student use
_____ Student take-home papers
_____ Make it/take it crafts
_____ Worship resources
_____ Teaching aids packet
_____ Music resources, cassettes, CDs, song books
_____ Audiovisual material like videos, CDs, computer software
_____ Other (specify) _____

7. Other criteria

There are other criteria that are important to the life of a church that should be considered when choosing a curriculum. (Some examples are provided. Add your own.)

_____ Adaptability of material for the small membership church
_____ Ease of use by the teachers
_____ Artwork and story illustrations are inclusive of all God's people
_____ Denominational identity, heritage, mission, and values are important
_____ Opportunities for mission and service outreach
_____ Cost
_____ Other (specify)

Curriculum Materials Evaluation Checklist

General Design

1. Content:
   a. What are the stated goals of this curriculum material? Do they match the goals we have set?
   b. Does the material help us reach our goals?
   c. Is the Bible translation used familiar to our people?
   d. Does the biblical material reflect an acceptable approach to biblical interpretation?
   e. How is biblical material used (for example, as a proof text for an idea or to raise critical questions)? What are the advantages and disadvantages of this approach to the Scriptures for our context?
   f. How appropriate is the material in terms of its interpretation of the meaning of the Christian life?
   g. Is the content appropriate to the age level, developmental issues, learning abilities, and life experiences of our people?

2. Arrangement of the material:
   a. How do we rate the material in terms of its physical appearance? Is the format of the materials attractive?

b. What is the structure of each session? How are the sessions related to one another? Is this an appropriate structure for our setting?

c. Is there space for additions and substitutions where appropriate? If so, are there suggestions for such additions and substitutions?

3. Can our congregation afford this material? Can it be used again?

Teacher Materials

1. Are the sessions clearly outlined so that a teacher can understand the movements of teaching?

2. What kinds of teacher helps are provided? Is material about the age, learning levels, needs, and interests of the students provided? Is there background material about the content so that the teacher's knowledge and understanding will be enriched?

3. How well does this material match our teachers' skills?

4. Are instructions for activities clear and easy to follow?

5. Are the resources we want and need provided? What resources are suggested for use beyond those provided? Which of these are essential? Are they easily obtained?

Student Materials

1. From the student's perspective, is the material attractive? Is printed material easy to read? Does the style and language attract the student's interest? Is the given material within the student's understanding?

2. Are the students engaged in the learning process in ways appropriate to their ages, learning abilities, needs, and interests?

3. What kinds of activities are used? Will the activities attract their interest? Will the students find these activities useful? Are these activities appropriate to the content?

Concluding Question

Weighing the advantages and disadvantages, is this an appropriate and useful curriculum resource for our church? State the reasons why or why not.

A P P E N D I X   4

Selected Bibliography of Curriculum Resources for the Small Membership Church

Sunday School Resources

The Best Whole People of God Online!: Check out this simple, easy-to-use curriculum at www.wholepeopleofgod.com. A very reasonable annual subscription provides flexibility, especially for small congregations.

Bible Quest: Order from www.biblequestlink.com. This curriculum has a multiage resource.

Gather 'round: Hearing and Sharing God's Good News: Order from www.gatherround.org/index.php. This is a curriculum project of the Church of the Brethren, Mennonite Church Canada, and Mennonite Church USA. It includes a multiage component.

One Room Sunday School: Order from www.cokesbury.com. The title says it all!

Seasons of the Spirit: Order from www.spiritseasons.com. This curriculum has a multiage resource.

Workshop Rotation: Visit www.rotation.org for lots of information about this adaptation of the learning center approach. Free lessons are available that can be adapted for small church use. Check out the article on using the WoRM model in the small church.

www.sundaysoftware.com: Even small churches can have computers. This is a good website for finding excellent software (CDs and DVDs) for use in your educational ministry.

Intergenerational Resources

Generations Learning Together by Donald and Patricia Griggs (Nashville: Abingdon Press, 1980): An oldie but a goodie in terms of resources.

Growing Together: A two-volume resource with intergenerational activities designed for use throughout the church year. Order from www.livingthegoodnews.com.

Live, Learn, Pass It On! by Patty Meyers (Nashville: Discipleship Resources, 2006): This book provides a practical overview of multigenerational learning.

Websites

www.elca.org/christianeducation/programs/: This Evangelical Lutheran Church in America website provides tips and resources for intergenerational events.

www.ncccusa.org/elmc/family2005/index.html: This is a resource for intergenerational events in the church.

Books

Chromey, Rick. *Children's Ministry Guide for Smaller Churches.* Loveland, Colo.: Group, 1995.

Griggs, Donald L., and Judy McKay Walther. *Christian Education in the Small Church.* Valley Forge, Pa.: Judson Press, 1988.

Ray, David R. *The Big Small Church Book.* Cleveland: Pilgrim Press, 1992.

———. *The Indispensable Guide for Smaller Churches.* Cleveland: Pilgrim Press, 2003.

———. *Wonderful Worship in Smaller Churches.* Cleveland: Pilgrim Press, 2000.

APPENDIX 5

Selected Bibliography of Children's Literature

Alexander and the Horrible, Terrible, No Good Day by Judith Viorst (New York: Simon and Schuster, 1972). With humor, Viorst describes a very bad day in the life of a child. If you ever need a book to go with a Job text, this might be the one.

All Things Bright and Beautiful by Cecil Alexander (New York: Harper Trophy, 2004). This book is an illustrated version of the hymn and could be used when the hymn is being sung, or on a day when Creation is the focus of the scripture.

Before You Were Born by Nancy White Carlstrom (Grand Rapids, Mich.: Eerdmans, 2004). This book celebrates the birth of a new child and the changes that come in the family. It can be used with Psalm 139:13-16.

Bread Bread Bread by Ann Morris (New York: HarperCollins, 1993). A picture book of different kinds of bread from around the world. It is excellent for World Communion Sunday.

Bright Star, Bright Star, What Do You See? by Cassandre Maxwell (Minneapolis: Augsburg Fortress, 1990). This tells the Christmas story.

Does God Hear My Prayer? by August Gold (Woodstock, Vt.: Skylight Paths Publishing, 2005). This delightful book asks some of the questions that children ask and then provides some answers. The illustrations are wonderful.

Does God Know How to Tie Shoes? by Nancy White Carlstrom (Grand Rapids, Mich.: Eerdmans, 1993). In a creative manner

Carlstrom asks questions about God and, in the answers, engages
children as they journey in faith.

The Easter Story by Allia Zobel-Nolan (Pleasantville, N.Y.: Reader's
Digest Children's Publishing, 2004). The story is taken from Mark
11–16 and is quite faithful to the Gospel story. There are good illustrations.

Families of God by Susan S. Swartz (Minneapolis: Augsburg Fortress,
1994). This book talks about how all people around the earth are in
the family of God.

Follow the Star with the Wise Men by Stephanie Jeffs (Nashville:
Abingdon Press, 2001). This is a good telling of the visit of the Magi.

For Heaven's Sake by Sandy Eisenberg Sasso (Woodstock, Vt.: Jewish
Lights Publishing, 1999). Rabbi Sasso is an excellent writer for children. This story is about a little boy who kept hearing the phrase "for
heaven's sake" and decided to look for heaven. After asking several
people, he goes to visit his grandmother, and they look together.

The Friendly Beasts by Sharon McGinley (New York: HarperCollins,
2000). This book illustrates the hymn. It would work well when the
hymn is sung during worship.

Giving Thanks by Jonathan London (Cambridge, Mass.: Candlewick
Press, 2003). This is a wonderful book for Thanksgiving or Earth Day.

God in Between by Sandy Eisenberg Sasso (Woodstock, Vt.: Jewish
Lights Publishing, 1998). A town searches for God, and God is found
in the in-between. The story is based on 1 Kings 11–12.

God's Paintbrush by Sandy Eisenberg Sasso (Woodstock, Vt.: Jewish
Lights Publishing, 1992). This book helps children understand who
God is. The illustrations are beautiful.

Good News Travels Fast! by Lisa Flinn (Minneapolis: Tandem Library
Books, 2003). This is the Easter story told through the eyes of those
who heard the news.

Growing in Faith: Seven Stories for Children by Helen Caswell
(Nashville: Abingdon Press, 1998). This book is a compilation of
seven stories: "God Is Always with Me," "God Makes Us Different,"
"God Must Like to Laugh," "God's Love Is for Sharing," "I Can Talk
to God," "I Know Who Jesus Is," and "My Big Family at Church."
The one negative of these stories is that inclusive language is not
used, but this can be corrected by the reader.

Horton Hatches the Egg by Dr. Seuss (New York: Random House,
1940). Here, in one of the delightful books by Dr. Seuss, the theme
is faithfulness, and Horton epitomizes this.

I Can Pray with Jesus by Debbie Trafton O'Neal (Minneapolis: Augsburg Fortress, 1997). This is a book that explains the Lord's Prayer to children.

I See the Moon by Kathi Appelt (Grand Rapids, Mich.: Eerdmans, 2004). This is a good book about the presence of God, with wonderful illustrations.

I Sing a Song of the Saints of God by Lesbia Scott (New York: Morehouse Publishing, 1991). This book illustrates the hymn and would be good to use on All Saints' Day as children are growing in their understanding of saints.

If I Had Lived in Jesus' Time by Peter Graystone and Jacqui Thomas (Nashville: Abingdon Press, 1995). This book shows daily activities as they would have happened in Jesus' time and compares them to activities in our time.

In God's Name by Sandy Eisenberg Sasso (Woodstock, Vt.: Jewish Lights Publishing, 1994). Another wonderful book by Rabbi Sasso, it talks about the many names of God and would go well with the Brian Wren hymn, "Bring Many Names."

Little Drummer Boy by Ezra Jack Keats (Minneapolis: Tandem Library Books, 2000). This book goes with the Christmas song and has superb illustrations.

March around the Walls with Joshua by Stephanie Jeffs (Greensboro, N.C.: New Day Publishing, 2007). This tells the story of Joshua and has good illustrations.

Martin's Big Words by Doreen Rappaport (New York: Hyperion Books, 2001). This is an excellent book about Martin Luther King, Jr. You might need to shorten the text slightly if you have primarily younger children.

Memories of the Manger by Michelle Medlock Adams (Nashville: Ideals Publications, 2005). The Christmas story is told by a dove to all of the animals in the barn.

Morning Has Broken by Eleanor Farjeon (Grand Rapids, Mich.: Eerdmans, 1996). This book wonderfully illustrates the hymn.

Raising the Roof by Roland Kidd (Americus, Ga.: Habitat for Humanity, 1995). This book tells the Habitat Story and can be used when your church takes part in a Habitat build.

The Runaway Bunny by Margaret Wise Brown (New York: HarperCollins, 1942). This story goes well with Psalm 139, reminding us that God is with us no matter where we go.

Sing Praise by Rhonda Gowler Greene (Minneapolis: Augsburg Fortress, 2006). This is a delightful story of Creation, told in rhyme with excellent illustrations.

Someone Very Special by Vickie Howie (Minneapolis: Augsburg Fortress, 2004). This contains stories about Jesus with particular attention to Jesus' death and resurrection. It is well done.

Someone's Come to Our House by Kathi Appelt (Grand Rapids, Mich.: Eerdmans, 1999). This celebrates a new baby. It could be used the Sunday after a new baby is born or as a gift to the family upon a new birth.

The Story of Ruby Bridges by Robert Coles (New York: Scholastic, Inc., 1995). This is the true story of the little girl who was in the forefront of desegregating schools in New Orleans. It ends with the prayer Ruby said several times a day during her ordeal.

Thank You, God by Sally Anne Conan (Mahwah, N.J.: Paulist Press, 1997). With delightful pictures, this book talks about the things children can be thankful for and ends with thanking God for creating me.

This Is the Lunch That Jesus Served by Dandi Daley Mackall (Minneapolis: Augsburg Fortress, 2006). This tells the story of the feeding of the five thousand.

Welcome Jesus by Carol Wehrheim (Cleveland: Pilgrim Press, 1997). This is a book for very young children. It very simply tells the story of Palm Sunday.

What Does the Sky Say? by Nancy White Carlstrom (Grand Rapids, Mich.: Eerdmans, 2004). Based on Psalm 19:1-4a, it invites a child to dream and wonder.

Where Is Jesus? by Sharilyn Adair (Nashville: Abingdon Press, 1997). A well-done book, it tells about Jesus and his parents going to the Temple and his parents' search for him.

Whoever You Are by Mem Fox (New York: Harcourt Children's Books, 2001). This is a book about likes and differences in this world. It has superb illustrations.

Wilfrid Gordon McDonald Partridge by Mem Fox (Brooklyn: Kane/Miller Books, 1989). A wonderful story about a little boy who helps an elderly woman find her memory.

Zacchaeus Has a Good Day by Sharilyn S. Adair (Nashville: Abingdon Press, 1997). This is the story of Zacchaeus, well told with good illustrations.

Notes

Introduction

1. Donald Griggs and Judy McKay Walther, *Christian Education in the Small Church* (Valley Forge, Pa.: Judson Press, 1988), 7.

1. The Lay of the Land

1. David R. Ray, *The Indispensable Guide for Smaller Churches* (Cleveland: Pilgrim Press, 2003), xi.
2. Gary Portnoy and Judy Hart Angelo, "Where Everybody Knows Your Name," *Keeper*, Arguntum label, 2003.
3. Ray, *The Indispensable Guide for Smaller Churches*, 51.
4. Ibid., 134.
5. Ibid., 139.
6. Karen B. Tye, *Basics of Christian Education* (St. Louis: Chalice Press, 2000). See especially chapter 2.
7. Caroline Westerhoff, "A Love Letter to People in Ordinary-Sized Churches," *Inside the Small Church*, ed. Anthony G. Pappas (Washington: Alban Institute, 2002), 108-9.
8. Lyle E. Schaller, *The Small Church Is Different!* (Nashville: Abingdon Press, 1982), 15.
9. Ray, *The Indispensable Guide for Smaller Churches*, 108.
10. Ibid., 110.
11. For a fuller treatment of this topic, see Karen Tye, *Basics of Christian Education*.
12. David R. Ray, *The Big Small Church Book* (Cleveland: Pilgrim Press, 1992), 96.
13. Ibid.

2. Who: It's All about People!

1. Robert Sylwester, *A Celebration of Neurons: An Educator's Guide to the Human Brain* (Alexandria, Va.: ASCD, 1995), 1.
2. Myrtle Felkner, "5 Ways to Do Christian Education in the Small-Membership Church." http://www.forministry.com/vsItemDisplay.dsp&objectID=81582639-A63E-4111-85C49A16B7FEF20C&method=display&templateID=C3435351-D45C-4B52-867A3F794D1CD85C (accessed August 2, 2006).
3. David R. Ray, *The Indispensable Guide for Smaller Churches* (Cleveland: Pilgrim Press, 2003), 55.
4. David R. Ray, *The Big Small Church Book* (Cleveland: Pilgrim Press, 1992), 93.
5. Ibid., 101-2.
6. Ibid., 102.
7. Ray, *The Indispensable Guide for Smaller Churches*, 133.

3. Where and When: Sunday School and Beyond

1. Myrtle Felkner, "5 Ways to Do Christian Education in the Small-Membership Church."
2. David R. Ray, *The Indispensable Guide for Smaller Churches* (Cleveland: Pilgrim Press, 2003), 137.
3. Ibid., 107.
4. David R. Ray, *The Big Small Church Book* (Cleveland: Pilgrim Press, 1992), 91.
5. When I use the term *events* in this chapter, I am referring not only to those single moments in time, like a fellowship dinner or a church-wide picnic; I'm also referring to experiences that occur over a period of time, like Advent, Lent, and vacation Bible school. All of these are events in the life of a congregation.
6. See Charles R. Foster, *Educating Congregations: The Future of Christian Education* (Nashville: Abingdon Press, 1994). Especially see chapter 2, for further discussion of "event-full" education.

4. How: Clues to Education in the Small Membership Church

1. There are various models to consider. See the Workshop Rotation Model in Neil MacQueen and Melissa Armstrong-Hansche, *Workshop Rotation: A New Model for Sunday School* (Louisville: Westminster John Knox Press: 2000); the shared Christian praxis approach in Thomas Groome, *Christian Religious Education* (San Francisco: Harper & Row, 1980); the story-linking approach in Anne Streaty Wimberly, *Soul Stories: African American Christian Education*, revised edition (Nashville: Abingdon Press, 2005); and the "event-full" model in Charles Foster, *Educating Congregations: The Future of Christian Education* (Nashville: Abingdon Press, 1994), to name a few.

2. See appendix 1 for a selected bibliography on models and methods.

3. Ray, *The Indispensable Guide for Smaller Churches*, 59.

4. See MacQueen and Armstrong-Hansche, *Workshop Rotation: A New Model for Sunday School*. Or check out www.rotation.org.

5. Carl S. Dudley, *Effective Small Churches in the Twenty-first Century* (Nashville: Abingdon Press, 2003), 86.

6. Wimberly, *Soul Stories: African American Christian Education*, revised edition.

7. See Richard L. Morgan, *Remembering Your Story: Creating Your Own Spiritual Autobiography*, revised edition (Nashville: Upper Room Books, 2002), for helpful resources for telling personal stories.

8. David Hogue, *Remembering the Future, Imagining the Past: Story, Ritual, and the Human Brain* (Cleveland: Pilgrim Press, 2003), 145.

9. This is adapted from the work of Carl Dudley, *Effective Small Churches in the Twenty-first Century*, 87-88.

5. Resources

1. David R. Ray, *The Big Small Church Book* (Cleveland: Pilgrim Press, 1992), 87.

2. Ibid., 98.

3. Ibid.

4. Barbara Bruce, *Our Spiritual Brain: Integrating Brain Research and Faith Development* (Nashville: Abingdon Press, 2002), 93.

5. David R. Ray, *The Indispensable Guide for Smaller Churches*, (Cleveland: Pilgrim Press, 2003), 148.

6. To locate samples, check with denominational resource centers, contact your area's denominational leaders, visit denominational and publisher websites, and check with other churches in your area who may have the materials.

7. I am deeply grateful to my friend and colleague Ann Schroer for letting me adapt a much larger bibliography she developed for a class on children in the church at Eden Seminary.

6. Guiding Principles

1. Caroline Westerhoff, "A Love Letter to People in Ordinary-Sized Churches," *Inside the Small Church*, ed. Anthony G. Pappas (Washington: Alban Institute, 2002) 109.

2. Donald Griggs and Judy McKay Walther, *Christian Education in the Small Church* (ValleyForge, Pa.: Judson Press, 1988), 7.

3. Walter Brueggemann, *The Creative Word* (Philadelphia: Fortress Press, 1982), 1.

4. Thomas Groome, *Christian Religious Education* (San Francisco: Harper & Row, 1980), 274.

5. Myrtle Felkner, "5 Ways to Do Christian Education in the Small-Membership Church."

6. David R. Ray, *The Indispensable Guide for Smaller Churches* (Cleveland: Pilgrim Press, 2003), 98.

7. Anthony G. Pappas, *Entering the World of the Small Church* (Washington: Alban Institute, 1988), 90.

Postscript

1. *Desert Wisdom: Sayings from the Desert Fathers*, trans. Yushi Nomura, introduction by Henri Nouwen (Maryknoll, N.Y.: Orbis Books, 1982), 24.

2. Lao Tzu, *Tao Te Ching*, trans. Edwin Sha, http://www.utdallas.edu/~edsha/tao1.html (accessed October 13, 2007).

3. David R. Ray, *The Big Small Church Book* (Cleveland: Pilgrim Press, 1992), 220.